What are the Other Kids Doing? ...while you teach small groups

Written by
Donna Marriott

Illustrator:
Gwen Connelly

Editor:
Joel Kupperstein

Project Director:
Carolea Williams

Table of Contents

Introduction

It is widely accepted that teaching and learning are best facilitated when instruction is delivered to the smallest possible group. The inevitable question is *While I'm working with a small group, what are the other 25 students doing?* While you could have "others" work alone, silently completing worksheets, a more student-centered scenario can be realized through independent literacy centers. The purpose of this book is to present a program of meaningful, manageable, and independent activities to involve students during small-group reading instruction. This program, called "Literacy Workshop," is designed to fill a 90–120-minute period each day.

Carefully crafted independent literacy centers have multiple advantages. Most importantly, they give teachers large blocks of uninterrupted time to work with small groups of students. I spend nearly two hours each morning working with different groups of three to seven students. I use this precious time for direct teaching, engaging students in a variety of rich literacy activities (guided reading, guided writing, modeled writing, shared reading, and literacy discussions). I have organized my time so that I meet with all four of my reading groups (called "Book Clubs") every day for about 25 minutes each. When they are not meeting with me, students work with the self-directed learning centers. In addition to facilitating small-group teaching and learning, these centers create ongoing opportunities for one-on-one instruction, individualized conferences, and both formal and informal assessment.

For children, literacy centers are an invitation to independent learning. While I'm teaching in our "Book Nook," other students are learning to take responsibility for their own education by exploring, responding, recording, constructing, practicing, and applying the skills of literacy through developmentally appropriate processes and activities. I expect my students to make significant and authentic decisions—what they will learn, with whom they will learn, and how long they will spend learning. With careful planning and clearly defined expectations, students can be set up to succeed. Each literacy center is designed to satisfy three rigorous criteria—independence, sustainability, and meaningfulness. Meeting these requirements ensures that students will enjoy and benefit from these activities over long periods of time.

Independence

The explicit goal of the teacher in this program is to work uninterrupted with small groups of students. This necessitates a parallel goal—students must be able to manage and complete the literacy center work independently. If they have to interrupt a small group to ask *How do you do this?* or *Will you help me?* or *What does this say?*, the teacher is unable to optimize teaching time. A variety of support structures is embedded within this program's activities and processes to facilitate students' independence.

- Centers are open-ended, offering multiple entry points, multiple paths to solutions, and multiple outcomes.

- Centers encompass an interesting and broad range of learning options.

- Centers are developmentally appropriate.

- Centers accommodate different learning styles.

- Centers are designed to emphasize and require application rather than to teach new skills. Most instruction occurs during the small-group meetings.

Sustainability

These literacy centers are intended to last for a complete year or, in some cases, multiple years. Because of the flexibility, longevity, and durability of these centers, the time you take preparing them will be time well spent. Students are expected to self-select literacy centers that are appropriate and interesting to them. Therefore, the centers you implement should be appropriate and interesting to as many students as possible throughout the year. For example, a very cute Thanksgiving project that takes three hours to format and prepare as a center might only be selected by three students during the course of the week. In other words, the amount of time spent developing thematic, holiday, and other "cute" centers may be disproportionate to the actual learning experienced by students. This doesn't mean you shouldn't do cute art projects—just don't offer them as independent centers. If you are going to spend three hours preparing a movable paper turkey with multicolored tail feathers on which children write five reasons they are thankful, you will want every single student to do the project, and you'll want a bulletin board display out of the deal! A better alternative is to present this sort of project in a whole-group format rather than a center format.

Meaningfulness

The purpose of these literacy centers is not just to keep children busy or quiet. The explicit purpose of this program is to offer activities that require students to understand, apply, and extend the curriculum. Every literacy center has been carefully created to ensure that it

- engages students in meaningful learning experiences.

- supports literacy goals.

- addresses the benchmark skills commonly specified in most district language arts performance standards.

- empowers students to employ their reading, writing, listening, and speaking skills.

After experimenting with literacy centers for several years, I solved some of the logistical, managerial, and curricular issues that you, too, may face as you move toward small-group and individualized instruction. The program, ideas, and activities in this book can be adopted in their entirety, adapted to fit any primary classroom, adjusted to your comfort level, or implemented one piece at a time. My sincere hope is that this resource is robust enough to offer something to each member of a very diverse audience.

5

Literacy Workshop—How It Works

READING TICKETS

Students carry customized Reading Tickets in a two-pocket folder to guide them through the Literacy Workshop. These Reading Tickets, the student contracts of the Workshop, are divided into three sections representing the program components—Have-To's, Once-a-Weekers, and Choices. After a student shows you a satisfactorily completed activity, sign off the activity on the Reading Ticket by writing your initials in the appropriate box. This book offers two Reading Tickets—one for independent students (page 23) and another for less independent students (page 22).

Reading Tickets serve four primary functions:

1. They allow you to set an individualized learning agenda for every student and ensure that every student engages daily in significant and appropriate learning activities.

2. They allow you to assess what students have accomplished during the week— what choices they made, how they paced themselves, and who helped them. Reading Tickets play a significant role in the weekly assessment of students' learning and your teaching. They are critical for keeping students accountable.

3. They ensure daily feedback on the core pieces of learning—independent reading, independent writing, and small-group instruction.

4. They allow students to work independently.

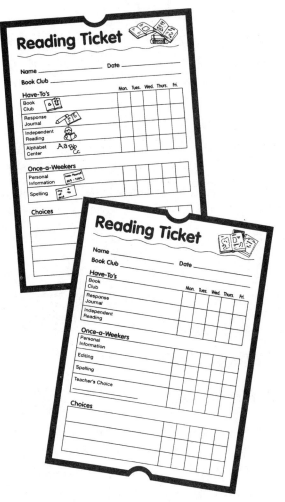

Though both Reading Ticket versions include the three program components, there are some significant differences between the two. The Reading Ticket for students who are less independent includes supportive illustrations and an additional Have-To—the Alphabet Center. The small pictures on this version help even the least advanced students "read" their Tickets independently. The pictures make it less likely that students will interrupt your small-group teaching time with questions such as *What do I do next?* or *What does this say?*

The only other significant difference between the two Tickets is the number of Once-a-Weekers required. Start less independent students with just one Once-a-Weeker—Personal Information. (Every child, no matter how young, should know his or her name and phone number.) Introduce spelling as the second Once-a-Weeker requirement only when students begin to make sense of how letters and sounds make words. A child cannot be expected to spell words he or she can't read! Once students demonstrate mastery of the Alphabet Center and understand the Reading Ticket system, they can "graduate" to the more independent Reading Ticket.

■ Have-To's

Student choice is a fixed and key element of the Literacy Workshop. Of course, with complete freedom, there is the possibility that a student may choose to not do any centers or do the same center repeatedly. Have-To's are a safeguard against this. Every student must complete Have-To's every single day before beginning any literacy centers. Even if students spend the entire period on Have-To's to the exclusion of other center choices, they will still gain the skills to become successful readers, writers, thinkers, and doers.

Even though Have-To's are nonnegotiable, students should still have opportunities to make authentic choices. For

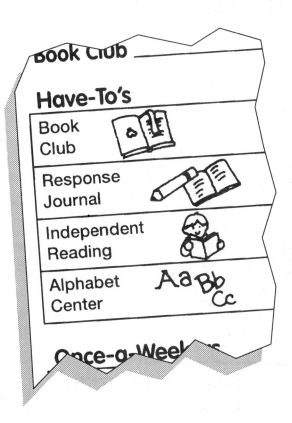

example, ask students to decide what to write about and how much to write in their response journals. For independent reading, invite each student to decide what to read, how many books to read, and with whom to read. In Book Clubs, be sure to embed authentic, important choices into the experience, including how to respond to literature and, when possible, invite students to decide which titles to read. The four Have-To's include small-group instruction (Book Clubs), Response Journals, Independent Reading, and Alphabet Center (for some students) as described on the following pages (8–12).

♦ Book Clubs

Book Clubs offer you the opportunity to lead small groups of students through developmentally appropriate, in-depth studies of literature. Book Clubs can vary in size from three to eight children and should include a heterogeneous mix of emergent, early, and fluent readers. Because Book Clubs are truly the heart of the Literacy Workshop, be sure to meet with each group daily. Maximize the teaching/learning potential of the Literacy Workshop by using the literacy centers, management tips, and assessment ideas to engage students in independent, meaningful learning activities while you work with your Book Clubs.

The overarching objective of Book Clubs is to help students develop understanding of reading as a meaning-making process. Book Clubs should take young readers beyond issues of simple decoding. Through Book Clubs, readers should learn to

- discuss literature with insight and sophistication.
- respond to literature in a variety of formats and contexts.
- take increasing responsibility for the depth, direction, and pace of their own learning.

Be sure that your Book Club lesson plans are crafted for students rather than focused only on the literature.

Develop plans for each piece of literature to address the individual needs of students, to respond to the unique "personality" of the reading group, and to meet the criteria of your language arts framework. By definition and design, Book Clubs should be varied in approach, sequence, and content. For example, a short picture book lesson may be completed in a week and rely on considerable teacher support. A chapter book lesson, on the other hand, may take a month and be designed around peer support and independent research projects. When designing Book Club lessons, try to include

- reading mastery and comprehension as the goal.
- an in-depth study of the book.
- shared and guided reading.
- literary discussion.
- skills development.
- a parallel study of poetry.
- writing.
- collaborative or individual projects.

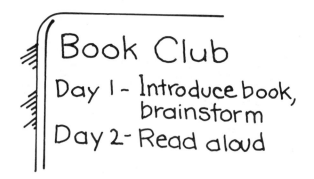

Book Club
Day 1 - Introduce book, brainstorm
Day 2 - Read aloud

♦ Response Journals

Response journals are ongoing written conversations between you and each student. Have students write to you every day, and write a note back to them every evening. This may take a bit of time (30–45 minutes daily), but the advantages are so rich that the time investment is worthwhile. Response journals allow you to

- assess every student's writing ability.

- create additional opportunities for individualized guided reading and writing on an as-needed basis.

- personalize writing experiences to "fit" each child.

- get to know each student personally.

- watch each student's writing improve over the course of an entire school year.

Spiral-bound notebooks can be used as response journals, but unfortunately, these tend to fall apart midway through the school year. It takes considerable time and yards of duct tape to make the journals last until the end of the year. You may find traditional composition books to be a sturdier alternative.

It is easy to individualize learning in response journals. At the beginning of the year, you might write to a student *Do you live near school?* Straightforward yes-or-no questions engage even the most reluctant writers. Quickly move away from the yes-or-no format by guiding developing writers to use environmental print. If you have a color-word poster, for example, you might write *What color are your shoes today? Mine are black.* If you have posted a list of weather words somewhere in the room, you might write *What kind of weather do you like best?* Another strategy for supporting emergent writers is to supply the

actual words they might need within a question. For example, *What kind of ice cream do you like best? Vanilla, choco-late, or strawberry?* Also, very early on, encourage writers to use other students' names. For example, *Who did you play with at recess yesterday? or Who is wearing blue shoes today?*

> 10:1 You have pink shoes? How pretty! Do your shoes have shoelaces?
>
> ☑ yes
>
> ☐ no
>
> 10.2. Are your shoelaces white?

Over time, students will move away from these contrived exchanges toward more conversational pieces on self-selected topics.

> 9·3·96 How was your mom's birthday? What did you do on her birthday?
>
> ⊖ THE YOUSH EAT CAKE OPEN PRASINTS
> oh... usual you wo

You can respond to the more detailed conversations of advanced writers by asking relevant questions or sharing similar personal experiences to propel the next day's writing.

> What is the scariest ride you have ever seen in your whole, entire life? at the fair I have went on a hamer-head ride. It was fun and scary at the same time. What ride are you taking about in san Diego Detroit I went to thme

Some students may even wish to co-author a story in their journals.

> 10·2 Once upon a time, in Lion Country safari, a baby lion ... Was born. He Jumps and plas With his cusins and brother and Sistrs. ¹⁰⁺³ His older brother, Sam, was teasing him one day. Sam said, "I'm going to ...ll your tail tonight while yo...

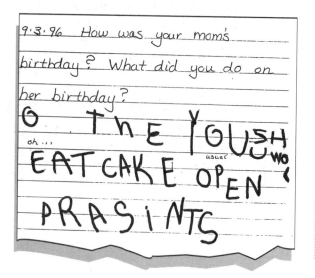

Others like to work on their interviewing and reporting skills.

> *Tomorrow I'd like you to go interview Ms. W. Today I'd like you to come up with 5 (or more) questions to ask Ms. W*
>
> **What is your favorit color?**
> **Wich do you like better reading or writing?**
> **Why do you like cats ~~so~~ much?**

But how do you engage students who cannot yet read or write independently? If you have a parent volunteer, cross-age tutor, student teacher, or student aide, have him or her help students read your responses and provide "grown-up" writing. If you have no help whatsoever, here are a few suggestions:

- Spend ten minutes helping children read their response journals before starting your first Book Club. Spend another ten minutes at the end of the workshop adding "grown-up" writing to children's approximations. You will need to shorten your Book Clubs slightly to be accessible for this support, but if your students are that dependent, 20-minute Book Clubs are appropriate.

- Only write to half the class each day.

- Use a different kind of daily writing. Response journals work well, but they are not the only option for daily writing. Instead, you could begin with whole-class journal prompts and move individual students toward response journals as they demonstrate appropriate levels of confidence and competence. You might also consider having students respond to each other. Partner them in advance (changing the pairings every few weeks) or have them randomly pick journals to read and respond to.

♦ Independent Reading

Students need regular, sustained opportunities to practice reading at every stage of the learning continuum. Therefore, independent reading is integrated into every student's Reading Ticket. Even though independent reading is a daily requirement, students still have considerable and significant decisions to make, such as what to read, with whom they read, where to read, and how many books to read.

Students record all the books they read on an Independent Reading form. This book includes three different forms. The first form (page 24) is designed for the earliest readers. The lines are spaced far apart, and there is room for only dates and titles. The next form (page 25) requires more information from the reader. Readers need to indicate if they have read books alone or with a friend. (As students move toward reading independence, they should read alone more frequently.) The most demanding Independent Reading form (page 26) asks students to rate books and indicate genres. Invite students to select the forms they feel are right for them. In most cases, they will choose appropriately.

Because students must make decisions about the type of books they read, you may want to organize and label your classroom library. Recommended

categories include nonfiction, poetry, songs, award winners, fiction, alphabet and number books, featured authors, and folktales. By separating books, even if the categories are somewhat unconventional, students are encouraged to read more broadly.

Have students each keep their current Independent Reading forms with their Reading Tickets in their two-pocket folders. When forms are filled, have students place them in a "Done Tray." These completed forms will be rich with important assessment data. They will show

- how many books a child reads daily.

- if a child is reading familiar or unfamiliar texts.

- if a child is choosing appropriately challenging materials.

- what kinds of books each child likes to read.

♦ Alphabet Center

The clearest indicators of early reading success are ownership of the alphabet and development of phonemic awareness. Students who need more support with these critical skills should be required to visit the Alphabet Center daily. It is essential that this center be "manned" by a student teacher, aide, parent volunteer, cross-age tutor, or more advanced peer. You can have children work alone endlessly tracing letters, spelling out their names with dough, or listening to cassette tapes of alphabet songs with very little impact. You will need an adult or more advanced peer to help these students make the links between letters and sounds. The support can be as simple as *This is the letter* c. *It sounds like* /c/. *Let's see if we can think of some words that start with* c. Have student aides help at the Alphabet Center for no longer than ten minutes so they, too, have time to do their own work.

Offer a variety of activities at the Alphabet Center and change them regularly to respond to the growing needs of your students. Activities may include

- letter/sound matching—Concentration, Bingo (page 54).
- letter recognition—writing letters with chalk, making alphabet books, cutting letters from magazines and newspapers.

- sound/symbol correspondence—matching beginning letter sounds to classroom objects, making "sewing cards" (threading yarn through hole-punched index cards to form letters).

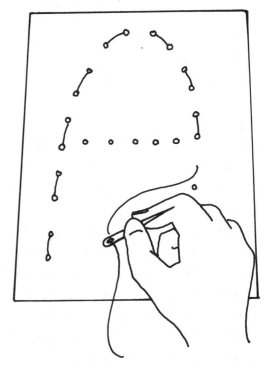

As students advance, you may want to offer activities designed to help them improve their skills with final consonants, medial sounds, rhymes, word families, blends and digraphs, and sight words. The Alphabet Center needs to grow with your students, and it should not be the only time that you work with phonemic awareness, letter-sound connections, or phonics. This is simply a way to include these skills as regular components of the Literacy Workshop.

■ Once-a-Weekers

In addition to Have-To's, several other important activities are critical to children's literacy development. These activities, though important, would be tedious if done every day. Completing each of the four activities once a week will adequately meet students' needs.

Once-a-Weekers include Personal Information, Spelling, Editing, and "Teacher's Choice." Ideally, students should do one of these each day, but if you let them take responsibility for their own pacing and scheduling, you may see some revealing learning patterns emerge. Ambitious personalities work feverishly on Monday to do all their Once-a-Weekers. They like to get these requirements out of the way and are willing to sweat blood to do it. Logical, sequential children do one activity a day, often proceeding right down the list from top to bottom. Then there are the procrastinators who wait until halfway through the Literacy Workshop on Friday and shift into panic mode to complete all four pieces. Be tolerant of all time-management styles. Inviting students to take responsibility for their own pacing encourages them to understand their unique learning styles and work strategies. This may have long-lasting implications both in school and the "real" world.

♦ Personal Information

At the beginning of the year, to model size, spacing, and alignment, write each student's full name, address, and phone number on lined paper. Glue these papers to sturdy tagboard and laminate. Place the paper in each student's Literacy Workshop folder. At first, you may wish to make less-independent students responsible for only their names and phone numbers. When they demonstrate mastery of these, add their complete addresses.

This activity has two learning objectives:

- Every student needs to know his or her name, phone number, and address. This is not only a real-life skill, it could also be a survival skill!

- Students need regular opportunities to practice forming letters accurately on lined paper. Although it may not be necessary for all students, many need structured practice to form letters properly.

Although you cannot tell by looking at student work if every letter has been formed correctly, you will be able to see if letters are aligned properly. Work on letter formation at another time during the day. When signing off a Reading Ticket, ask the student to recite his or her personal information. When students can write and recite their personal information perfectly, move them to more challenging and appropriate learning experiences. For these "graduates," simply cross out "Personal Information" on the Reading Ticket and substitute a more appropriate activity.

Cory Jarrett

174 Mill Dr.
Rossmoor, CA 90720

555-4638

♦ Spelling

Because students have diverse abilities, they should not have to practice the same spelling words at the same time. Nor should they take one uniform spelling test simultaneously. The spelling component of your Literacy Workshop program should be flexible and oriented to each student's developmental needs.

To create an individualized spelling program, assemble a list of 200 high-frequency words ordered from least difficult to most difficult. (Research-based, commercially published word lists work well, too.) Based on these

words, make spelling cards geared to three levels:

Level 1: Each card has five words and moves the student through the first 30 words.

Level 2: Each card has ten words and moves the student through the next 70 words.

Level 3: Each card has ten words and moves the student through the remaining 100 words.

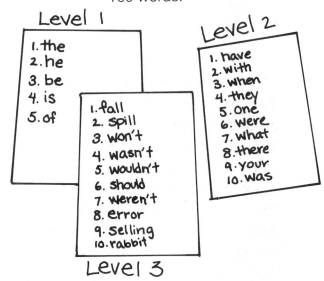

Level 1
1. the
2. he
3. be
4. is
5. of

Level 2
1. have
2. with
3. when
4. they
5. one
6. were
7. what
8. there
9. your
10. was

Level 3
1. fall
2. spill
3. won't
4. wasn't
5. wouldn't
6. should
7. weren't
8. error
9. selling
10. rabbit

Create a list of all 200 words and staple a copy inside each student's two-pocket folder. This is an essential feature of the spelling component of the Literacy Workshop. Weekly tests do not ensure that students will spell correctly in their daily writing. Anyone familiar with the traditional "Friday spelling test" approach will attest to this. Just because children spell words right on a test does not mean they know them! The big spelling list (all 200 words) allows you, the student, and classroom helpers to know at a glance which words the student must spell correctly. The daily expectation that owned words must be spelled conventionally guides children toward increased spelling mastery. When a child asks for a sign-off on a response journal, you can use the big spelling list to make sure that "owned" words have been spelled properly. If these words have been misspelled, don't sign the student off until the words have been corrected. Have students start this spelling program only when they are developmentally ready. Once students understand how letters and sounds are used to form words, give them the first spelling card.

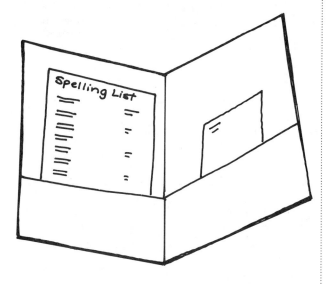

To conduct spelling tests, have a cross-age tutor or adult helper test five or six students each day, one at a time, on the words on their spelling cards. When a child owns a word, have the tutor highlight that word on the student's spelling card and big spelling list. When a student owns all the words on a card, give him or her the next card. Have students store their current spelling cards inside their two-pocket Literacy Workshop folders. This particular format is simple and effective, but you will, of course, deliver your spelling tests in a way that is comfortable for you, reasonable for your children, and responsive to your specific classroom context.

It is important to note that the spelling component of the Reading Ticket is not a spelling test. It is, instead, a structured opportunity for students to practice their own spelling words. Each of the following four formats students can choose for spelling practice has specific teaching/learning objectives. Encourage students to try all four formats over the course of the year.

Try/Copy/Try: Have students find a spelling partner to give them a practice test. Then, have them copy their spelling words correctly, comparing the conventional spelling with their initial try. Finally, have them cover the words one at a time and try again. This format is beneficial because two students work together to complete the project. Have students use the recording form on page 27 for this project

Word Shapes: Have students write their spelling words on the recording form (page 28). Next to each word, have them draw the word "shape." As an intermediary step, students can write their words directly on the grid before coloring the boxes. This activity helps children visualize each word's shape and is especially helpful for visual learners.

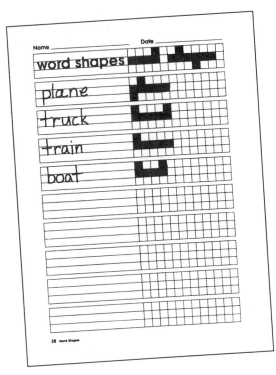

Rainbow Letters: Have students use a different color (crayons or colored pencils) for every letter in the word. This format helps students see words one letter at a time. Invite them to use paper of their choice for this project.

Double Words: Have students copy their spelling words twice, each time using a different crayon or colored pencil. The objective is to practice the whole word—to see the sequence of letters as a whole unit. Using two colors makes the repetition less tedious. Invite students to use paper of their choice for this project.

♦ Editing

There are two levels of editing activities. The introductory level reproducible, Get It Right! (page 29), provides space for an incorrect sentence and a lined response area for students to rewrite the sentence correctly. At the end of each incorrect sentence, indicate how many errors the student needs to find. The objective is not to trick students; you want them to find all of the errors. The advanced editing task reproducible, Edit It! (page 30), is similar to Get It Right! but provides space for three sentences. As students progress, increase the difficulty of their editing work. Indicate on each student's Reading Ticket whether he or she should do Get It Right! or Edit It!

♦ Teacher's Choice

The final Once-a-Weeker allows you to direct students toward specific literacy centers that are normally part of the Choices section of the Reading Ticket. Because students may choose to visit any learning center they want, they may choose to avoid certain centers. Teacher's Choice allows you to make sure there are no gaps in a student's learning experience, to move each student toward balanced learning, and to individualize the learning program to benefit each student. For example, if you notice that a student needs practice with dictionary skills and has not experienced Digging through the Dictionary (page 80), you might use Teacher's Choice to direct him or her there. Once noted as Teacher's Choice, the center is a requirement!

■ Choices

Students may proceed to Choices activities each day only after they have been signed-off for their daily Have-To's. Have them use any remaining time during the Literacy Workshop to work on Choices. Allow students to decide whether or not to complete Once-a-Weekers before they proceed to Choices. This book describes 30 independent literacy centers that can be used as Choices. These centers have been carefully designed to address discrete skills and learning objectives expressed in most district language arts performance standards.

Display a menu of literacy centers in a pocket chart by writing the name of each center on a cut-apart sentence strip and attaching a supporting illustration (hand-drawn, cut from catalogs, or photographs of actual centers). Invite students to refer to the menu when selecting Choices or copying activity titles onto their Reading Tickets. Including illustrations in the menu is vital for emergent and early readers, and though it may take a bit of time to prepare the display, you will make up for it later by gaining long, uninterrupted teaching time with your Book Clubs.

The numerous options help diffuse students and avoid traffic problems, so you should not need to impose people or time limits at any of the learning centers. Sometimes you may have a bit of congestion at Computers (page 75)—particularly if you are introducing new software. If this happens, simply add a kitchen timer to the center and let students solve the time problem themselves. This is a real-life learning experience that belongs in the hands of children. If students can't solve this kind of minor traffic problem, just turn off the computer. This same shut-down principle works any time a center is not being used properly. Be sure you are consistent with your expectations and with the consequences.

It is quite possible that you will not have the time or assistance to do sign-offs for Choices. Do not be uncomfortable with this management decision. Students get individualized conferences for their Have-To's and Once-a-Weekers each day. That means that someone is regularly giving students feedback on their core learning activities. Because the centers require students to leave a product or some "residue of learning," you will be able to assess their work and guide them toward the next learning episode.

SIGN-OFFS

Sign-offs are an integral part of the Have-To's and Once-a-Weekers. Sign-offs help ensure that children are stretching themselves academically and receiving whatever support they require. For a sign-off, the student shows his or her work to you (or to whatever adult might be in the room) for some input. Discuss the student's work, and if it is satisfactory, initial the Reading Ticket. These mini-conferences during sign-offs are opportunities for one-on-one teaching.

When a student asks for a sign-off for a response journal, you can briefly

- provide whatever "grown-up" writing is necessary.

- conduct guided writing to extend the piece or emphasize a certain learning point.

- check for spelling on the student's big spelling list.

- check to make sure the response addresses the question.

- check for legibility and fluency.

When a student asks for a sign-off for independent reading, you can

- ask the student to read his or her favorite page.

- ask the student to tell the story in his or her own words.

- check that the student chose an appropriate book or an appropriate number of books.

When a child asks for a sign-off for an editing task, you can

- ask why he or she put a period at the end.

- check to make sure new sentences are entirely correct.

Any project that requires writing needs to be checked for spelling and readability, whether or not it receives a sign-off. Many emergent writers may need "grown-up" writing on their work. In a multiage classroom, older students can provide this assistance. If you're lucky enough to have a parent volunteer, cross-age tutor, student teacher, or classroom aide, he or she can provide "grown-up" writing. If you have no extra help,

- display lots of environmental print.

- provide "word walls."

- designate "center buddies" (a stronger reader/writer supporting a weaker reader/writer).

- shorten Book Clubs by five minutes and provide sign-offs between each group. (Target less independent writers to get the most accomplished.)

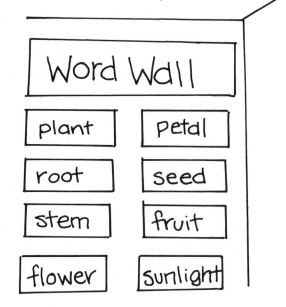

Sign-offs offer built-in opportunities for regular, individualized, and meaningful assessment. This daily feedback loop is a vital ingredient in nudging students toward continuous progress. Here are some tips for managing sign-offs:

- Don't spend much time on each sign-off. Sign-offs should usually take from several seconds to a minute.

- Don't try to do sign-offs and Book Clubs at the same time. Set a rule that, unless they need immediate ambulance service, students may not interrupt Book Clubs. If you are the only adult in the room, be sure students know to hold onto their work until you finish with the current Book Club.

- Plan ahead for times when you have no extra help. At the beginning of the Literacy Workshop period, assist your least independent learners in reading their response journals. (That is really the only piece that sometimes needs a bit of support before children can get to work.)
  At the end of the Workshop, reserve a little time to do sign-offs. If pressed for time, concentrate on your least independent learners. Later, you can check everyone's response journal, Independent Reading form, and Once-a-Weekers.

- Ask for parent volunteers. Train volunteers in what to look for and how to respond gently and positively to student work. Parents can do these sign-offs wonderfully well (as can student aides, classified support staff, cross-age tutors, and other volunteers).

- If you have absolutely no time or help, don't do the sign-offs! Have students check themselves off as they complete each task. You can check the core pieces—Have-To's and Once-a-Weekers—later. Most literacy centers (Choices) also require students to leave concrete products you can assess at a later

time. If you are able to individually touch each learner through daily sign-offs, go for it. If not, go for the next best thing. It's easy to think of reasons we can't change our learning programs—no extra help, limited supply budget, too many at-risk learners, not enough room, not enough materials, too many kids, district constraints. The greater challenge is to design the most provocative learning program for each child in spite of these obstacles.

Reading Ticket

Name _____ **Date** _____

Book Club _____

Have-To's

	Mon.	Tues.	Wed.	Thurs.	Fri.
Book Club					
Response Journal					
Independent Reading					
Alphabet Center					

Once-a-Weekers

Personal Information					
Spelling					

Choices

What Are the Other Kids Doing While You Teach Small Groups? © 1997 Creative Teaching Press

Reading Ticket

Name _____ Date _____

Book Club _____

Have-To's

	Mon.	Tues.	Wed.	Thurs.	Fri.
Book Club					
Response Journal					
Independent Reading					

Once-a-Weekers

Personal Information					
Editing					
Spelling					
Teacher's Choice _____					

Choices

What Are the Other Kids Doing While You Teach Small Groups? © 1997 Creative Teaching Press

Independent Reading

Name _____

Date	Title

Independent Reading

Name _____

Date	Title	Shared	Read Alone

Independent Reading

Name _____

Date	Title and Author	Silently	Shared	Rating (1, 2, 3, 4, 5)	Type of Book

Try/Copy/Try

Name _____   Date _____

Name _____ **Date** _____

word shapes

What Are the Other Kids Doing While You Teach Small Groups? © 1997 Creative Teaching Press

Get It Right!

Name _____

Date _____

Circle the mistakes. The number of mistakes is in parentheses. Then, rewrite the sentence correctly. Good Luck!

Edit It!

Name _____ Date _____

Rewrite these sentences correctly. The number of mistakes in each sentence is in parentheses. Good Luck!

Management

No matter how thoughtful or cute your literacy centers are; how many hours you have invested in designing and creating engaging learning activities; how much money you have spent on books, reproducibles, and materials; and how good your intentions are, if you do not have a management system that works, you're going to have problems— big problems. The management system described in these pages has been carefully developed. But keep in mind that a good management system needs to grow and change in response to students, classroom context, and teacher preference. You may need to make adaptations to match your comfort level and best meet the needs of your students.

This management system allows you to

- individualize learning.
- give students responsibility and authentic choice.
- provide a low-maintenance, user-friendly structure that students can manage independently.
- account for every student's learning throughout the Literacy Workshop period.
- work undisturbed with small groups of students.

GETTING STARTED

Getting started with literacy centers is not as hard as you might think. Initially, you may want to start small. Depending on your familiarity with independent learning centers, it may be unreasonable to implement 30 centers tomorrow, next week, or even next month. Just take one comfortable step at a time.

When introducing a new center, take two or three students who need that learning experience and make them "experts." Model the entire activity, complete it with these students, have them try it on their own, and reteach it as necessary. When other students are ready for this center, steer them to the experts for guidance.

Another way to introduce centers is directly through Book Clubs. If, for example, a group needs to work on writing summaries, introduce them to Book Review (page 61) as part of their group work. If the book being read by a Book Club presents an appropriate context for learning prefixes or suffixes, have the group work on Expand-a-Word (page 84). In this way, you can guide small groups of students toward specific learning episodes, revitalize student interest in a center, and review the processes and objectives of a center.

Introducing centers in a whole-group format is not usually recommended. However, if you find yourself starting a school year with 30 new students who are unfamiliar with the idea of independent centers, you might do a "big teach" of three easy-to-learn centers such as Listening Post (page 99), Make-a-Book (page 103), and Sticker Story (page 140). During this initial instruction, spend a good amount of time ensuring that students master these centers. Then, introduce a new center each week (or every other week) to the whole group, using student experts, or in Book Clubs.

TIME MANAGEMENT

With time, practice, and trust, students learn to assume responsibility for their learning. Do not impose time limits on students' center activities. A no-time-limit scenario acknowledges every student's unique learning strengths, needs, and interests. Time limits can lead to what has been called the "Cha-Cha" curriculum. The teacher sets a time limit, moving groups of students to the next activity at some predetermined signal—work, work, cha-cha-cha, work, work, cha-cha-cha. Scheduled group rotations is a management strategy that appears orderly—all students complete the learning agenda—and it can reduce the noise and activity level. However, children do not necessarily learn in an orderly, uniform, lockstep manner. Allowing students to pace themselves respects and celebrates their individual learning needs.

Also, refrain from imposing people limits at centers whenever possible. In most cases, students can take care of traffic problems on their own. Since students select their own activities and determine their own schedules, learning groups are heterogeneous and very fluid. Such groups are more often defined by interest than by ability, age, or gender. These are important decisions to put into the hands of young children!

CLASSROOM ENVIRONMENT

Even if you don't have a lot of extra space in your room, you can still have literacy centers. Most of the centers in this book can be kept in small plastic containers and stored almost anywhere. Directions can be laminated or inserted into plastic display stands and placed in the containers. If space is an issue, centers may not be the problem—it may be your classroom furniture. You might want to reconsider what furniture is absolutely necessary for learning and which pieces are dispensable.

The optimal classroom for independent learning may challenge some pervasive paradigms. For example, does every student really need a desk? There is no indication that students learn better sitting at individual desks. Some students seem to learn just as well sprawled out on the floor. Since a truly independent program includes virtually no whole-group teaching, students seldom need to sit at desks at the same time. However, there should be enough nooks, crannies, and chairs available so all students can be seated at the same time, if necessary. Also, three or four individual desks should be tucked away into quiet corners for students who prefer to work alone. Since these are not "assigned" seats, occupants may change, depending on the time of day and the activity. A variety of tables tucked into learning areas works quite well also.

You may also want to consider letting go of your teacher's desk. In an independent-learning program, you will rarely find yourself sitting in it, and teachers' desks are simply enormous! Instead, use a smaller table placed against a wall.

Also, consider letting students work outside (if you are fortunate enough to have access, proximity, and cooperative weather). A picnic table just outside the door makes a quiet, tranquil, inviting work space. It is crucial, if students work outdoors, to have windows that allow you to keep them in sight.

This is a diagram of an effective setup for an independent-learning classroom. Keep in mind that this is only one example.

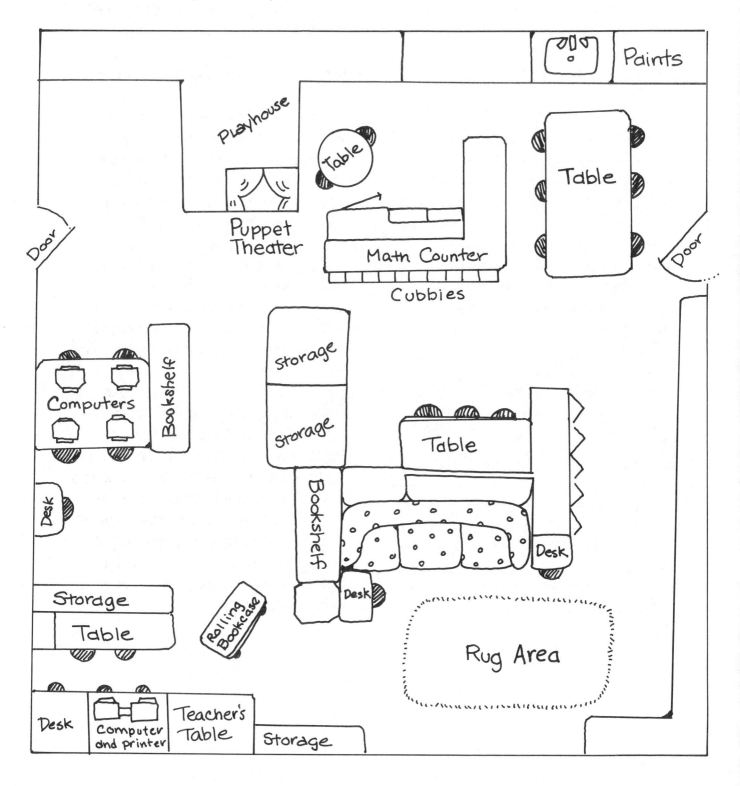

STORAGE AND PRESENTATION

Each literacy center is a collection of resources. The size, presentation, and storage of centers will vary depending upon the resources you use.

Most centers in this book are not fixed or location-specific. Materials can be assembled in a plastic tub or basket, and students can work on the activity in any available space. Label each center's container with large laminated index cards bearing the center name and a picture. Store the containers wherever there is counter or shelf space. It will take students little time to learn where the containers are.

You may find that some activities work better as stationary centers. Many activities can even be presented as wall displays! For example, Stamp Collecting (page 137) is quite effective presented as a poster. And Map Attack (page 105) works well when the maps are attached to a wall. Wall centers are often most effective when displayed in corners because they take up less surface area and are out of the way.

Because of required materials, some centers clearly cannot be moved. Computers, listening posts, typewriters, and overhead projectors must be kept near electrical outlets and usually stay in the same place throughout the school year. Whenever possible, have these centers do "double duty." For example, by shrinking your Listening Post (page 99) to two or three terminals and removing headsets, this center can double as a workplace. An overhead projector can serve two centers—Light Write (page 97) and Overhead Projector (page 123). A pocket chart also provides space for both Book Match (page 59) and Build-a-Sentence (page 68).

Most centers require recording forms or other reproducibles. For some of these centers, it's best to have the necessary forms right at the center. Typically, these are half-sheet forms that fit in small plastic baskets. Most recording forms, however, are best presented in multicompartment organizers. Inexpensive, durable cardboard organizers can be found at many office-supply or department stores. Label each compartment by inserting a sheet of construction paper with a labeled flap that extends beyond the edge. Write on this flap the name of the form and include an illustration so less independent readers can find what they need. Also, use a variety of colored construction paper in the compartments to help students get around this classroom "office." Students can read the different labels, or find activity forms according to color (e.g., red for Digging through the Dictionary forms, green for Thesaurus forms).

For personal storage, each student should have two classroom cubbies—a work cubby and a "take-home" cubby. If your students have individual desks, these can serve as their work cubbies. Multicompartment organizers make effective cubbies as well. Students can keep all their Literacy Workshop materials in their work cubbies, including the two-pocket folders that hold their Reading Tickets (pages 22–23), Independent Reading forms (pages 24–26), spelling cards, response journals, and any ongoing work. Students can store work that is ready to be taken home in the take-home cubbies. Be sure students check their take-home cubbies each day before they leave.

In an independent-learning classroom, a communal approach to supplies and materials works well. Keep pencils, glue bottles, scissors, construction paper, paper scraps, tissue paper, staplers, tape, yarn, writing paper, paper clips, and erasers at a single supply station. Because your objective is to work with small groups without interruption, even the placement and availability of materials should allow students independent access and management.

BEHAVIOR MANAGEMENT AND CLEANUP

As in every learning program, there needs to be appropriate consequences when students do not meet their learning responsibilities. You will want to establish your own system to implement these consequences. If you stay in the classroom during recess to do assessment and preparation, consider letting students stay in with you to "catch up." Do not present this option as a punishment. Simply tell students *If you need more time to finish your work you may stay in at recess.* Learning to self-pace can be quite difficult for young children. However, with patience and consistency, most students quickly learn to manage their time efficiently and effectively.

A program with 30 centers can make quite a mess! Be sure to establish a cleanup routine as soon as you introduce the centers. For example, give every child a classroom job that changes monthly. Make sure that every area of the classroom is someone's responsibility. Use a simple set of general cleanup instructions, such as *Clean up your mess, Do your job, Help a friend.* If your schedule allows, end the Literacy Workshop right before recess or lunch. This provides impetus to the cleanup process since, of course, the room must sparkle before anyone can leave.

Cleanup List

Chalkboard — Noelle
Bookcase — Roger
Coatrack — Kyang
Art Supplies — Sandra
Pocket Chart — Melinda
Reading Corner — Armando
Alphabet Center — Julia
Sink — Phillip
Blocks — Jamaal

Assessment

DAILY ASSESSMENT

Students need immediate and meaningful feedback in order to make continuous progress. This kind of systematic assessment is an integral feature of the Literacy Workshop. The core pieces of learning—Have-To's and Once-a-Weekers—require sign-offs, ensuring that every student receives daily, one-on-one feedback. These brief, personalized conferences provide ongoing opportunities to validate learning, assess progress, and nudge students forward.

During sign-off conferences, students share their work with you. These conferences might last from several seconds to a minute or two. Initiate this sort of interaction with students needing extra help with reading—whether it is decoding, comprehension, or expression. A longer conference might sound like this:

Student: *Will you sign me off for independent reading?*

Teacher: *Let me see your recording form. You used good, clean handwriting today, and you wrote the date properly. Wow! Did you enjoy reading* The Three Billy Goats Gruff?

Student: *Yes.*

Teacher: *Did you read the story all by yourself or did you read with someone today?*

Student: *I read the book with Sean.*

Teacher: *Buddy reading is a good strategy when you're trying out a hard book. Will you read me your favorite page?*

A shorter sign-off conference (with a more advanced student) might proceed this way:

Student: *Will you sign me off for independent reading?*

Teacher: *What did you read today?*

Student: *I read* The Three Billy Goats Gruff.

Teacher: *Tell me one thing you liked about the story.*

Student: *I liked it when the Troll was knocked over the bridge.*
Teacher: *Did you feel sorry for the Troll?*
Student: *No, he was mean and got what he deserved.*

If you are lucky enough to have extra help in your classroom (a student teacher, cross-age tutor, parent volunteer, or classroom aide), ask them to conduct these sign-off conferences. That will leave you free to concentrate on your small groups. Remember, ideally, you are setting up an independent learning environment so you can teach small groups without interruption.

Daily assessment is also promoted by interacting with the actual products of learning. Check students' Have-To's and Once-a-Weekers daily to assess how they are doing and what you need to do to urge them forward. The most intimate daily assessment opportunity is the response journal. Read each student's response journal every day. Though you may typically use these journals to "chat" with students, don't hesitate to assess and encourage students. For example, your response might read *This was a bit hard to read. Please try skipping lines tomorrow. Okay? Now, please tell me more about your new bike,* or *Wow, you wrote so much today! Good work! Do*

you think your dog will ever learn to stop barking at the next-door neighbor?

So you can assess literacy center activities, have students put completed work in a "Done Tray" (unless the work is wet or gluey, in which case have children set it aside to dry). Look at these papers each day after school. If you find something that requires direct teaching, make a point to spend a minute or two with that student the next day. For example, if Rachel turns in an Alphabetizing (page 49) form that is not in alphabetical order, plan to spend some time with her. If a piece is turned in that has been done carelessly, return it to the student to redo. For example, when Paul, whom you know understands ending punctuation, turns in an Edit It! (page 30) piece without periods, just hand it to him as he walks into class the next day and ask him to edit his Edit It! Most of the work in

Done Tray

the Done Tray should be correct because students have engaged in sign-off conferences. They have already briefly shared their work with you or another adult and worked out the bugs. File student work in folders and store the folders in a child-friendly cabinet—short and easy to open. Students sometimes need to check work from a previous day; make this easy for them. If a child claims, "But I already did my Personal Information!", you can respond, "Well, go look in your file for it and show it to me." If you store completed work in a place that students cannot access, then the responsibility of checking for missing or questionable work becomes yours. This should not be your responsibility—you should concentrate on teaching.

WEEKLY ASSESSMENT

There are three strategies for getting a broader look at each student's weekly progress. One is the Reading Ticket itself. At the end of each week, take out each student's Reading Ticket and check for the following:

- Were the learning tasks completed?

- Who signed off the student's completed tasks? (If a student is always signed off by a cross-age tutor, you will want to investigate.)

- Which centers did the student choose?

- How is the student managing and pacing his or her learning? (It is interesting to see how students pace their Once-a-Weekers, for example.)

Also, look at each student's Independent Reading form at the end of the week. Check to see

- how many books the student read each day.

- if the student is reading familiar or unfamiliar material.

- if the student is reading a variety of genres (poetry, nonfiction, student-made books).

- if the student is reading appropriately challenging materials.

Leave notes directly on the forms, such as *This book is too easy, Please read more than one book a day,* or *Wow, you are making good choices!* Students should know that you look at their forms every week and often have important feedback.

The third strategy involves recording each student's Choices on a tally sheet (page 44). These tally sheets list all 30 center options and hold 20 weeks of data. Write each student's name and starting date on a tally sheet and store the sheets in a three-ring binder. This allows you to track students' Choices over time to determine learning patterns and gaps.

Name Elliot	Tally				
	9/10	9/11	9/24	10/1	10/8
Alphabetizing	X	X			
Bingo					
Book Match	X				
Book Review					
B's and D's			X		X
Build-a-Sentence	X	X	X	X	
Computers					
Creation Station					

Based on this assessment data (the completed Reading Ticket, the Independent Reading form, and the tally sheet), prepare new Reading Tickets for the next week. If necessary, leave notes for students on their Reading Tickets. For example, if you notice that a student is establishing a pattern of reading one easy book a day, write *Please read two or three books each day* or *Read more challenging books, please.* Use the Teacher's Choice option (under Once-a-Weekers) to ensure a balanced learning program. For example, if you notice on the tally sheet that a student has not done Build-a-Sentence (page 68), indicate this as Teacher's Choice. If, in checking a response journal, you notice consistently incomprehensible writing, write on the Ticket, *Only (your name) may sign off this week.* That guarantees that you will have time with this student each day for additional guided writing.

How long does all this take? You will probably need to spend about an hour each week reviewing and preparing Reading Tickets. You'll find it time well spent. The weekly assessment format allows you to direct each student to the next learning activity. It comes close to true individualized teaching.

MONTHLY ASSESSMENT

At the end of each month, invite students to look through the file folders that hold their day-to-day work. Ask each student to select pieces that demonstrate growth and add these to a personal portfolio. Have students complete and staple a WOW! form (page 45) or a Self-assessment form (page 46) to each piece. (Invite students to choose the reflection form they feel is appropriate.) This process follows the fundamental goals of portfolio assessment—collect, select, and reflect. Send the rest of the work home *en masse* for families to enjoy.

Although portfolio assessment is the focus of the monthly assessment program, try to incorporate it into daily assessment as well. Remind students to add pieces to their portfolios any time they do something worthy of a WOW! form. If you see something fabulous in the Done Tray, tell the student that it looks like a WOW! piece; invite the student to write a reflection and put it in his or her portfolio.

One suggestion for making portfolios is to use pizza boxes. Ask a local pizzeria to donate medium-size boxes. Have students decorate the boxes during the first week of school to give a sense of ownership right from the beginning. Store the boxes on a shelf in the front of the classroom in tidy stacks. Students can easily take their boxes from the stack, open them up to see their work, and return their boxes to the stack. At the end of the year, invite students to take their pizza-box portfolios home.

Compile students' Reading Tickets and send them home at the end of the month with other finished work (unless the Reading Tickets are selected for portfolios). Or, because Reading Tickets have rich assessment information, you may wish to file them in folders, using them to trace a student's learning pattern. These folders, however, often become bulky, need increasing storage space, and are quite cumbersome. Tally sheets are a more expedient way to see long-term learning. You might also consider sending Reading Tickets home at the end of each week to give families immediate feedback, but realize that this puts a lot of pressure on you to review old Tickets and prepare new ones on Friday! The once-a-month system for distributing Reading Tickets is recommended because it is comfortable and quite manageable.

Some work should not go into the completed-work file. Response journals, for example, are a yearlong process. Though you should make families welcome to peruse them at any time, the journals should stay in the classroom. At the end of the year, send them home in students' portfolios. Independent Reading forms also should not find their way into this file. Though children put their completed forms into the Done Tray, file them separately in their portfolios. As a set, these recording forms provide rich assessment data at parent conferences, revealing each child's emerging and deepening literacy profile. They are far less powerful when seen one form at a time.

YEARLY ASSESSMENT

Portfolios allow students to recognize their own growth over time. You may find that when students look at their work from the beginning of the year, they are surprised by their progress. It's not uncommon for students to say, "I wrote that? It looks like baby writing!" Similar to physical growth, cognitive growth progesses slowly. Cumulative portfolios are analogous to marking a child's height on a door frame. Children can only recognize that they are growing if they can see where they have been.

Yearlong portfolios also allow parents to see growth over time. Just as a photo album provides visual memories, literacy portfolios document important learning memories. Single, isolated work samples are like the scattered photos that invariably find their way into our junk drawers. They are fun to look at, but we may not be able to remember who is in the picture, where it was taken, or what happened before and after. A portfolio is more like a video, documenting learning in a fluid, sustained manner.

At the end of the school year, invite students to share their learning portfolios with their families in student-led conferences. Have them narrate a tour through their portfolios to celebrate a full year of growth. These conferences are also excellent opportunities for your own self-evaluation. As you go over student work, look for ways to improve your instruction for next year.

Sept. 21

Nicholos Kim

4168 Oak St.

May 8

Nicholas Kim
4168 Oak St.

Tally Sheet

Starting Date _____

Name _____

CENTER

Alphabetizing																						
Bingo																						
Book Match																						
Book Review																						
B's and D's																						
Build-a-Sentence																						
Computers																						
Creation Station																						
Digging through the Dictionary																						
Expand-a-Word																						
Handwriting																						
Independent Writing																						
Let's Do Lunch																						
Light Write																						
Listening Post																						
Make-a-Book																						
Map Attack																						
Never-Ending Story																						
Newspaper																						
Overhead Projector																						
Post Office																						
Reading to Learn																						
Research																						
Stamp-a-Card																						
Stamp Collecting																						
Sticker Story																						
Tape-a-Story																						
Thesaurus																						
Typewrite Right																						
Word Games																						

Name _____ Date _____

WOW!

This belongs in my learning portfolio because

_____

_____

_____

_____

✂ ┈┈┈

Name _____ Date _____

WOW!

This belongs in my learning portfolio because

_____

_____

_____

_____

Self-assessment

Name _____ Date _____

The best thing about my piece is . . .

_____

_____

_____

_____

If I could change one thing it would be . . .

_____

_____

_____

I would rate my piece as . . .

Great!   Very Good   Okay   Yuck!

Literacy Centers Overview

Center	Objective	Benchmark Skill
Alphabetizing	Students read for literary and information purposes.	Alphabetize words to the first or second letter.
Bingo	Students use a variety of strategies to derive meaning from print.	Acquire sight vocabulary. Expand usage of high-frequency words.
Book Match	Students use a variety of strategies to derive meaning from print.	Master basic concepts of print (stable text, one-to-one word matching, directionality).
Book Review	Students show clarity in writing.	Sequence ideas and thoughts to retell a story.
B's and D's	Students read for literary and information purposes.	Alphabetize words to the second or third letter.
Build-a-Sentence	Students use a variety of strategies to derive meaning from print.	Use word lists and word banks to develop vocabulary. Expand high-interest vocabulary. Use noun–pronoun agreement, subject–verb agreement.
Computers	(Varies with software program.)	(Varies with software program.)
Creation Station	Students show clarity in writing.	Use descriptive language to write about experiences and impressions.
Digging through the Dictionary	Students read for literary and information purposes.	Use dictionary.
Expand-a-Word	Students use a variety of strategies to derive meaning from print.	Identify root words, prefixes, and suffixes.
Handwriting	Students generate written work that reflects knowledge of language conventions.	Print legibly and neatly with reasonable speed.
Independent Writing	Students see themselves as writers.	Understand and use the writing process.
Let's Do Lunch	Students read for literary and information purposes. Students develop speaking skills necessary for effective communication.	Use real-world resources. Recognize importance of reading in daily life. Speak appropriately in a variety of situations.
Light Write	Students generate written work that reflects knowledge of language conventions.	Print legibly and neatly with reasonable speed.
Listening Post	Students see themselves as readers.	Read for enjoyment. Self-select reading material.
Make-a-Book	Students use written expression to communicate for various purposes.	Write simple stories with beginning, middle, and end. Expand use of various forms of writing (personal experience, poetry, fiction, information, story expansion, autobiography).

Center	Objective	Benchmark Skill
Map Attack	Students read for literary and information purposes.	Use children's atlas and maps.
Never-Ending Story	Students read for literary and information purposes.	Demonstrate literal, interpretive, and critical comprehension. Show imagination and clarity in writing.
Newspaper	Students see themselves as readers. Students use written expression to communicate for various purposes.	Read challenging material. Use factual knowledge to relay information.
Overhead Projector	Students read for literary and information purposes.	Expand facility with a variety of genres (e.g., poetry, nonfiction, fantasy).
Post Office	Students use written expression to communicate for various purposes.	Expand use of various forms of writing (e.g., notes, invitations, friendly letters).
Reading to Learn	Students read for literary and information purposes.	Acquire across-curriculum content vocabulary. Use content-area books. Know parts of book (table of contents, glossary, index).
Research	Students utilize a variety of strategies to derive meaning from print. Students read for literary and information purposes. Students see themselves as readers. Students use written expression to communicate for various purposes.	Acquire across-curriculum content vocabulary. Use content-area books, library, word books, encyclopedia. Know parts of book (table of contents, glossary, index). Read challenging material. Use factual knowledge to relay information.
Stamp-a-Card	Students use written expression to communicate for various purposes.	Expand use of various forms of writing (e.g., notes, invitations, friendly letters).
Stamp Collecting	Students read for literary and information purposes.	Use children's atlas and maps.
Sticker Story	Students show imagination and clarity in writing.	Use descriptive language to tell about experiences and impressions of the world. Sequence thoughts and ideas.
Tape-a-Story	Students see themselves as readers.	Read aloud with expression and fluency.
Thesaurus	Students read for literary and information purposes.	Learn the purpose and use of a thesaurus.
Typewrite Right	Students generate written work that reflects knowledge of language conventions.	Move from estimated spelling to conventional spelling to convey information. Appropriately use capital letters and ending punctuation.
Word Games	Students utilize a variety of strategies to derive meaning from print.	Increase understanding of compound words and contractions.

Alphabetizing

Learning Objective

Alphabetizing words to the first or second letter

Materials

- ☐ index cards
- ☐ markers
- ☐ magazines
- ☐ glue
- ☐ scissors
- ☐ laminator
- ☐ plastic pencil box
- ☐ recording forms (pages 51–53)

Presentation and Storage

Create 30–40 word cards with initial letters spanning the entire alphabet. Draw simple illustrations or glue magazine pictures on the cards and laminate them for durability. (Consider making cards that students can alphabetize to the second letter as well.) Present the center in an inexpensive plastic pencil box clearly labeled with the activity title and a picture.

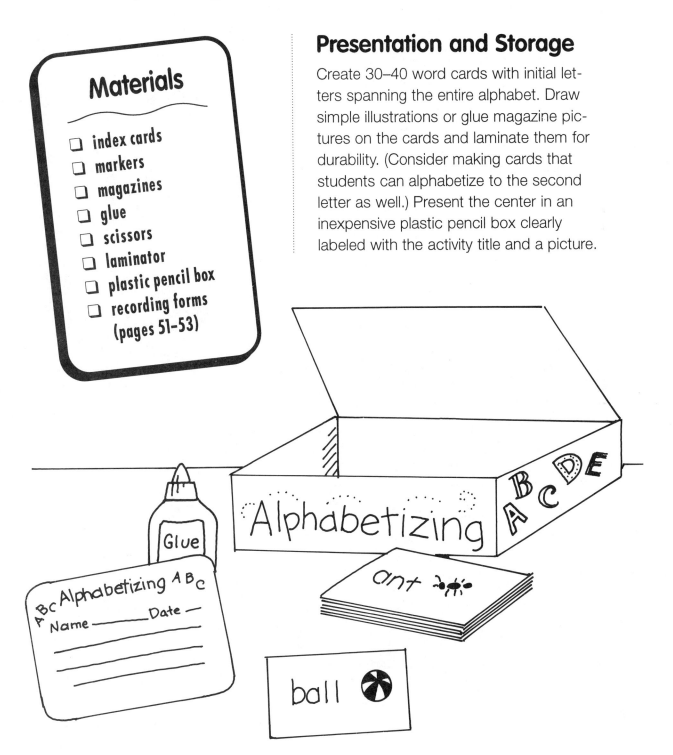

Process

The student selects cards randomly and arranges them in alphabetical order. Before recording, he or she has a friend check the work. (This way, two students are learning!) Finally, the student writes the word sequence on the appropriate recording form (pages 51–53).

Helpful Hints

Some students will be more successful starting out with only three or five cards and the recording sheets on page 51 and 52. For students who need a challenge, there is Super Alphabetizing (page 53), requiring students to alphabetize ten cards. The illustrations on the cards are very important for emergent and early readers. They should help even your earliest readers to work independently.

Alphabetizing ABCDEf

Name __Joel__   Date __Oct. 10__

1. __eye__
2. __igloo__
3. __kite__
4. __notebook__
5. __pumpkin__

Alphabetizing

Name _____ Date _____

1. _____

2. _____

3. _____

✂ ···

Alphabetizing

Name _____ Date _____

1. _____

2. _____

3. _____

Alphabetizing

Name _____ Date _____

1. _____

2. _____

3. _____

4. _____

5. _____

✂ ┈┈┈

Alphabetizing

Name _____ Date _____

1. _____

2. _____

3. _____

4. _____

5. _____

Super Alphabetizing ABC

Name _____ Date _____

1. _____

2. _____

3. _____

4. _____

5. _____

6. _____

7. _____

8. _____

9. _____

10. _____

Bingo

Learning Objective

Reinforcing sight recognition of high-frequency words

Materials

- word list template (page 57)
- scissors
- box
- game card template (page 56)
- sample word list (page 58)
- colored cardstock
- plastic basket
- resealable plastic bags
- plastic chips

Presentation and Storage

Using the word list template, create a composite word list based on the first 40 words of your 200-word spelling list (see page 15). You may also wish to use the sample word list on page 58 and make game cards from these words. Photocopy the word list, cut out each word, and place the words in a box. Create game cards by randomly choosing words from the word list and writing them in the boxes of the Bingo game cards. For durability, mount the cards on colored cardstock and laminate them. Present the center in a plastic basket and store cards in a resealable bag. Use plastic chips for markers and also store them in a resealable bag. Only fill the marker bag once. If students lose these, tell them they will have to figure out for themselves what to use for markers. Students will quickly learn to take care of the materials if there is an authentic consequence.

Process

Students use traditional Bingo rules to play this learning game. Though the game usually requires a minimum of two players, students can play alone. One student acts as the "word caller," picking words from the box and announcing them to the other players. A student playing alone may decide to be the word caller and play two or three cards simultaneously. These centers work best when as few rules as possible are imposed. If you make the learning objectives clear, provide the necessary materials, and leave the fine-tuning to the children, the desired learning will occur.

Helpful Hints

To make the game appropriate for a range of abilities, vary the difficulty of the words on the playing cards. Color-code the cards so students can choose appropriate difficulty levels.

- Green is a "go" for everyone.
- Yellow is a "caution"—the learning level is warming up.
- Red is "stop" and think—are you ready for a red-hot challenge?

Students can also create their own playing cards. Before beginning a game, have players select words from the word list to write randomly on blank game cards. For more advanced students or large student groups, include all 200 spelling words on the word list. This will increase the level of difficulty and decrease the probability of students having similar cards. The goal is that students learn to spell these words correctly and read them without hesitation.

Bingo Card

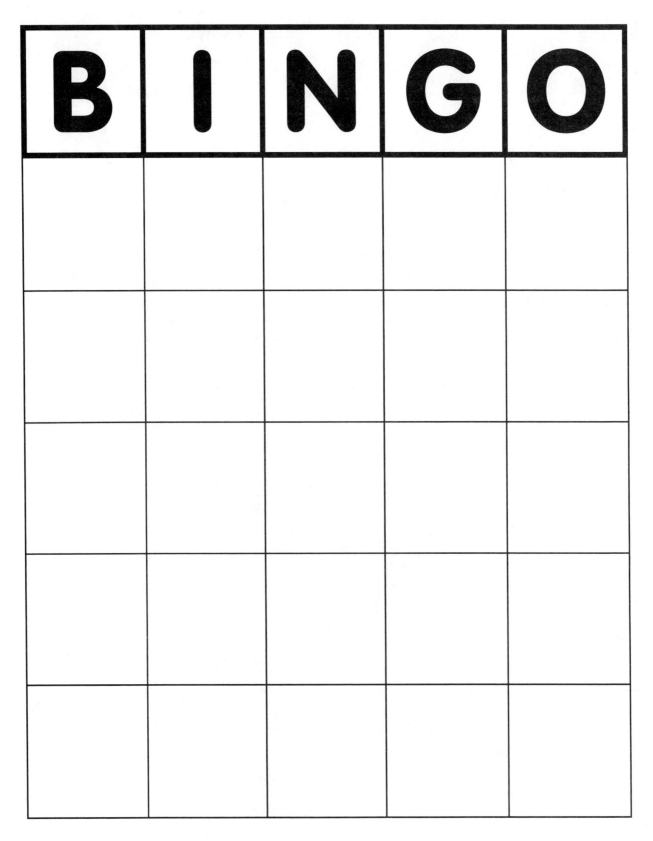

Word List

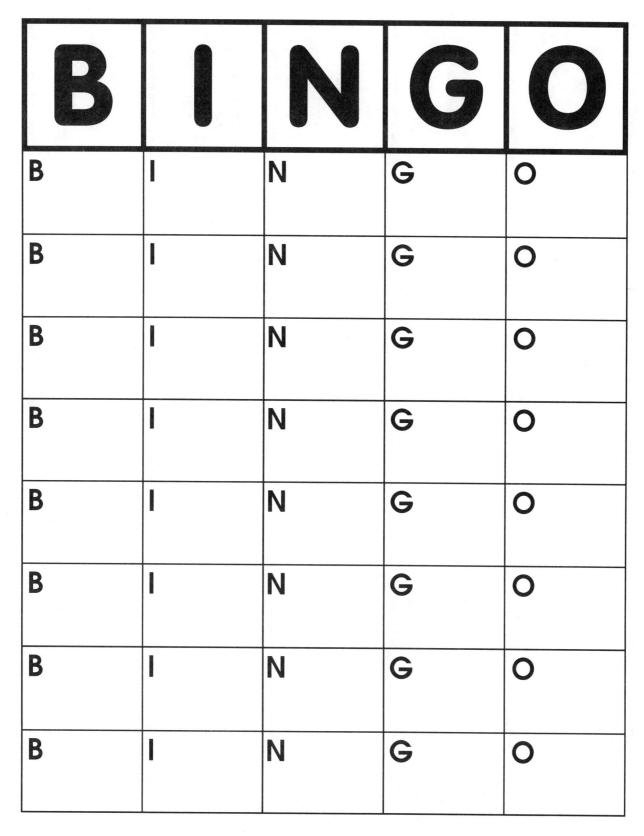

B	I	N	G	O
B	I	N	G	O
B	I	N	G	O
B	I	N	G	O
B	I	N	G	O
B	I	N	G	O
B	I	N	G	O
B	I	N	G	O
B	I	N	G	O

Sample Word List

B	I	N	G	O
B	**I**	**N**	**G**	**O**
the	he	be	is	they
B	**I**	**N**	**G**	**O**
of	for	this	you	at
B	**I**	**N**	**G**	**O**
and	was	from	that	by
B	**I**	**N**	**G**	**O**
a	on	I	it	one
B	**I**	**N**	**G**	**O**
to	are	have	with	had
B	**I**	**N**	**G**	**O**
in	as	or	his	not
B	**I**	**N**	**G**	**O**
but	what	all	were	when
B	**I**	**N**	**G**	**O**
we	there	can	an	your

What Are the Other Kids Doing While You Teach Small Groups? © 1997 Creative Teaching Press

Book Match

Learning Objective

Mastering basic concepts of print (word matching, word recognition, and identifying word boundaries)

Materials

- familiar children's books
- sentence strips
- scissors
- large resealable plastic bags
- tagboard
- plastic bin
- pocket chart

Presentation and Storage

Copy the text of a familiar book on sentence strips to provide additional reading opportunities without the support of illustrations. (Taking away the illustrations does not make a reading experience more valid, it just makes it different!) Cut the sentences into words, color-code each set, and store sets in resealable bags. (Color-coding makes it easier to return errant cards to their proper bags.) Put in the bag one copy of the book and a piece of tagboard labeled with the book title. Stand the bags upright in a plastic bin. By the end of the year, you may have 20–30 book bags, and you will definitely want them to last!

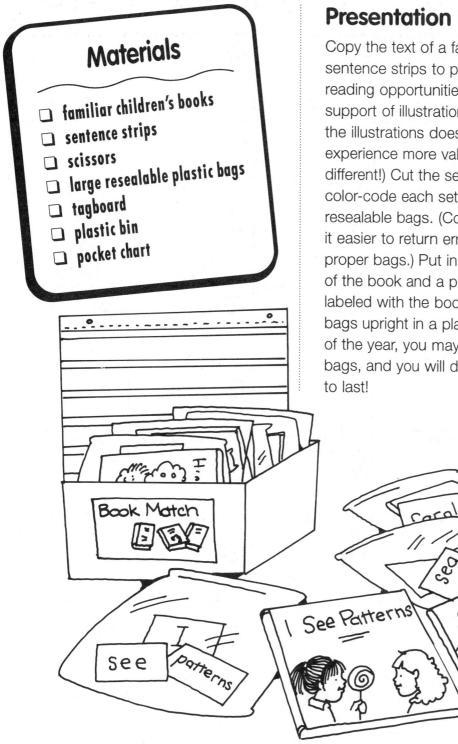

Process

Students arrange the words in a pocket chart using the book as a model. Once the story has been reconstructed, students read it to other students or to parent volunteers. This is one of the few learning centers that does not yield a product of student learning. You may ask students to leave the cards in place for you to check at a later time. However, you may prefer to have students pack up the cards as soon as they finish to keep the pocket chart free for other children. Once the book is read and reassembled properly, the student's learning goal has been reached.

Helpful Hints

Have students prepare sentence strips based on books from their Book Clubs. This will save you time and reinforce reading and writing. You may also wish to present text in this format when preparing to do a story innovation or copy-change.

This learning activity is most appropriate for emergent and very early readers. Once students are reading books that are 16 or more pages, they may have outgrown this activity. Also, if you have ever tried to reconstruct a long book one word at a time, you will probably agree that it is a very tedious process. Students who are reading longer texts need different learning opportunities.

Book Review

Learning Objective

Sequencing thoughts and ideas to summarize a story

Materials

- [ ] recording form (page 63)
- [ ] children's books
- [ ] art supplies (paints, crayons, oil pastels, colored chalk, colored pencils, markers, collage materials)

Presentation and Storage

This is an easy center to present. Provide students with recording forms, a library of children's books, and art supplies. Store the art supplies in a place easily accessed by children and keep recording forms in the classroom "office."

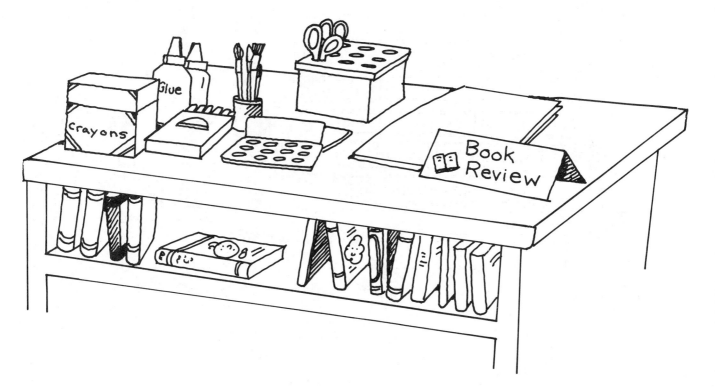

Process

Students each read a book and write a summary and recommendation on the recording form. So far, this center does not sound as though it has very much appeal, right? Here's the hook. Once they complete the recording sheets, invite students to illustrate their reviews with their choice of art supplies, including paints, crayons, oil pastels, colored chalk, colored pencils, markers, or collage materials. Display the completed reviews and illustrations in your classroom.

Helpful Hints

Giving students access to art supplies takes a bit of courage and some up-front training. For example, you may not wish to leave oil pastels out until you have taught students how to use them, how to store them, and how to clean up the mess they make.

Book Review

by _____

Title _____

Author _____

Summary

_____

_____

_____

_____

_____

_____

Recommendation

_____

_____

_____

_____

B's and D's

Learning Objective

Alphabetizing words to the second or third letter

Materials

- ☐ index cards
- ☐ markers
- ☐ magazines
- ☐ glue
- ☐ scissors
- ☐ plastic box
- ☐ recording forms (pages 66–67)

Presentation and Storage

Create a set of 30–40 illustrated word cards featuring only words beginning with the letters *b* and *d*. (Pictures cut from magazines make great illustrations. They work just as well as hand-drawn images and are much easier to make!) Present the center in a plastic box labeled with the activity title and a matching picture.

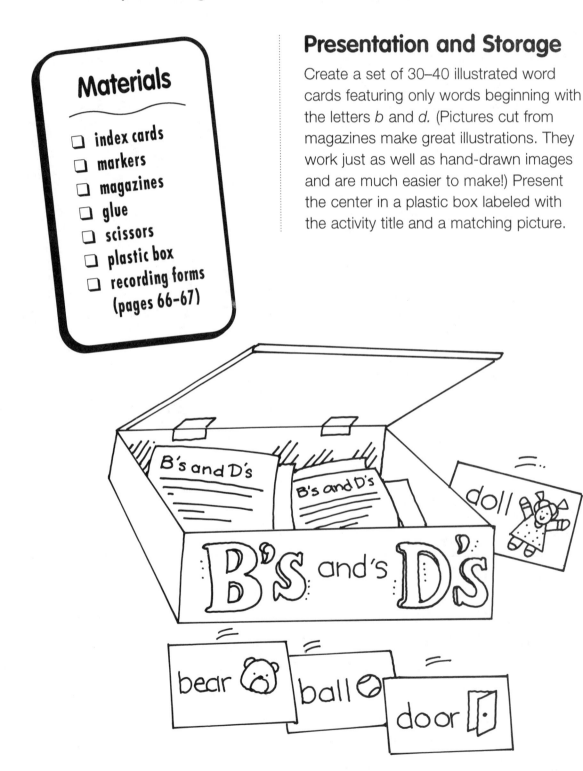

Process

Although the level of difficulty is higher, the process of this center is identical to Alphabetizing (page 49). Students select five random cards and arrange them in alphabetical order. Encourage students to have a friend check their work before they record it. Finally, have students record the alphabetized word list on the recording form (page 66).

Helpful Hints

This center is the next step for learners who have demonstrated mastery of Alphabetizing. Remember, centers need to allow for student growth. Once a student has clearly internalized a skill, he or she needs to be nudged toward more challenging learning. For your little wizards, try Super B's and D's. Using this form, children take ten cards instead of five and use the Super B's and D's recording form (page 67).

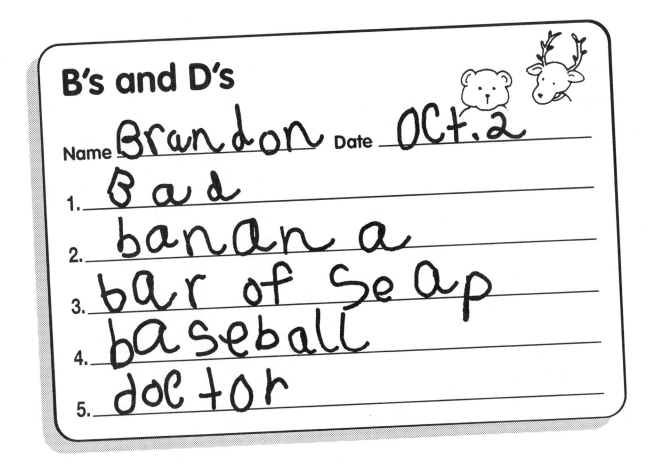

B's and D's

Name Brandon   Date Oct. 2

1. Bad
2. banana
3. bar of seap
4. baseball
5. doctor

B's and D's

Name _____ Date _____

1. _____

2. _____

3. _____

4. _____

5. _____

✂ ┈┈┈

B's and D's

Name _____ Date _____

1. _____

2. _____

3. _____

4. _____

5. _____

What Are the Other Kids Doing While You Teach Small Groups? © 1997 Creative Teaching Press

Super B's and D's

Name _____ Date _____

1. _____

2. _____

3. _____

4. _____

5. _____

6. _____

7. _____

8. _____

9. _____

10. _____

Build-a-Sentence

Learning Objective

Gaining awareness of parts of speech and sentence construction

Materials

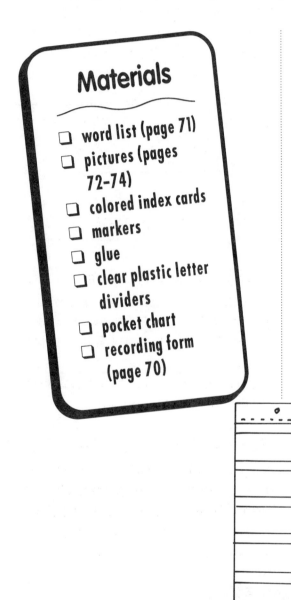

- [ ] word list (page 71)
- [ ] pictures (pages 72–74)
- [ ] colored index cards
- [ ] markers
- [ ] glue
- [ ] clear plastic letter dividers
- [ ] pocket chart
- [ ] recording form (page 70)

Presentation and Storage

Using the word list on page 71, create color-coded word cards. Write animal words on green cards, action words on red, describing words on orange, place words on yellow, and "in-betweeners" on white. Make a special *The/A* card by gluing two index cards together with *The* on one side and *A* on the other. Use the pictures on pages 72–74 to support each of the cards (except color words and in-betweeners). Leave a stack of blank cards so children can add cards. Keep the cards in clear plastic letter dividers labeled with the same color-coding system. Store all materials near the pocket chart.

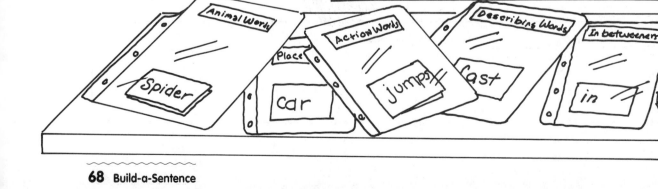

Process

Have students begin each sentence with the *The/A* card. This controls the sentence structure and ensures that the sentence will begin with a capital letter. Have students build complete sentences, read them to each other, and write them on recording forms. Look for unique twists students invent for this activity. Some may challenge themselves to make the longest, silliest, or hardest sentences. Some prefer to work alone, while others prefer to work together.

You may even see children try to make stories using all of the available words!

Helpful Hints

Categorizing words on colored cards helps children conceptualize (in an experiential format) how the parts of speech function. Pictures are absolutely necessary for engaging and supporting less independent learners. Encourage children who are not yet independent readers to arrange the cards in the color sequence below.

The/A * green word * red word * white word(s) * orange word * yellow word.

This sequence helps even the most limited readers arrange words into sentences. Write the sequence on a sentence strip and display it with the center materials. Have more fluent readers build longer, more complex sentences without referring to a color sequence.

Label the words *animal words, action words,* and *in-betweeners* rather than *nouns, verbs, articles, pronouns,* and *prepositions* to clarify word functions. If necessary, include standard labels with the words.

Build–a–Sentence

Name _____

Date _____

Build-a-Sentence Word List

Animal Words (green cards)

frog	spider	bee	cow
bear	sheep	turtle	walrus
goat	fish	bird	goose
rabbit	duck	cat	snake
chicken	rooster	camel	

Action Words (red cards)

eats	kicks	crawls	walks
sleeps	jumps	digs	runs
smiles	builds	drinks	stands
breaks	falls	hides	sits
pushes	cries	pulls	

Describing Words (orange cards)

white	green	fast
red	black	blue
yellow	little	big

Place Words (yellow cards)

road	phone booth	tree	gas station
house	library	car	bridge
mountains	kitchen	lake	garden
beach	circus	bookstore	tunnel
bedroom	nest	mailbox	

In-Betweeners (white cards)

the	they	with	on
a	in	some	to
and	at	this	I

What Are the Other Kids Doing While You Teach Small Groups? © 1997 Creative Teaching Press

Build-a-Sentence Pictures

What Are the Other Kids Doing While You Teach Small Groups? © 1997 Creative Teaching Press

Build-a-Sentence Pictures

Build-a-Sentence Pictures

Computers

Learning Objective

Objectives depend upon available hardware and software

Materials

☐ computer(s)
☐ software

Presentation and Storage

Supplies for this center will depend upon your school district's technology goals, your school's budget and spending priorities, the generosity of donors, and the availability of a "techie" to keep the system working. The presentation and storage will depend on the number of computers and printers you have available in your classroom (and the number of electrical outlets).

Process

Make computers available throughout your Literacy Workshop. Provide students with programs that address a variety of skills and abilities.

Helpful Hints

This is the only center that may have traffic problems. To help students solve these problems, place a kitchen timer at the computer center and suggest that, if a student wants to be next, the timer can be set to ten minutes. Require waiting students to continue learning while the timer does its job. Doing nothing should not be a choice. One timer for all of your computers still leaves lots of rich problem-solving opportunities for children.

Creation Station

Learning Objective

Using descriptive language to write about objects

Materials

- ☐ "junk" (cardboard tubes, clothespins, paper clips, broken toys, string, lids)
- ☐ large box
- ☐ art supplies (glue, paint, markers)
- ☐ recording form (page 79)

Presentation and Storage

This is an easy center to set up because all you need is a box of "junk." You might include cardboard tubes, clothespins, paper clips, scrap paper, broken manipulatives, string, microwave food trays, envelopes, and lids. If you ask students and their parents, friends, and relatives to collect junk, you will soon have more than you need. Place collected junk in a large box clearly labeled with the title and picture of the center or separate it into resealable bags.

Process

Invite students to use junk to make models or inventions. Students may construct rocket ships, mousetraps, playground equipment, plumbing systems, holiday gifts, pet supplies, storage facilities, computer gadgets, eating utensils, or stylish outfits. Have students write detailed descriptions of their materials, processes, and final products on the recording form.

Helpful Hints

Display finished creations in the classroom. If space is limited or if you want to reuse materials, just have children complete the recording form. Remember to periodically add new junk to the box if students don't reuse the materials.

Creation Station

Name _____ Date _____

Draw it! ➤

Describe it! ➤

Materials

Process

Product

Digging through the Dictionary

Learning Objective

Gaining familiarity with the function, structure, and use of dictionaries

Materials

- [ ] dictionary
- [ ] index cards
- [ ] markers
- [ ] self-pacing chart (page 83)
- [ ] hole punch
- [ ] three-ring binder
- [ ] recording form (page 82)
- [ ] plastic recipe box

Presentation and Storage

You will need at least one good, age-appropriate dictionary. Make about 40 numbered and laminated word cards appropriate for a variety of reading abilities. Place in a three-ring binder a copy of the self-pacing chart for each student. Store the cards and recording forms in a plastic recipe box and keep them next to your dictionary. Clearly label the box and binder with the activity title and a picture.

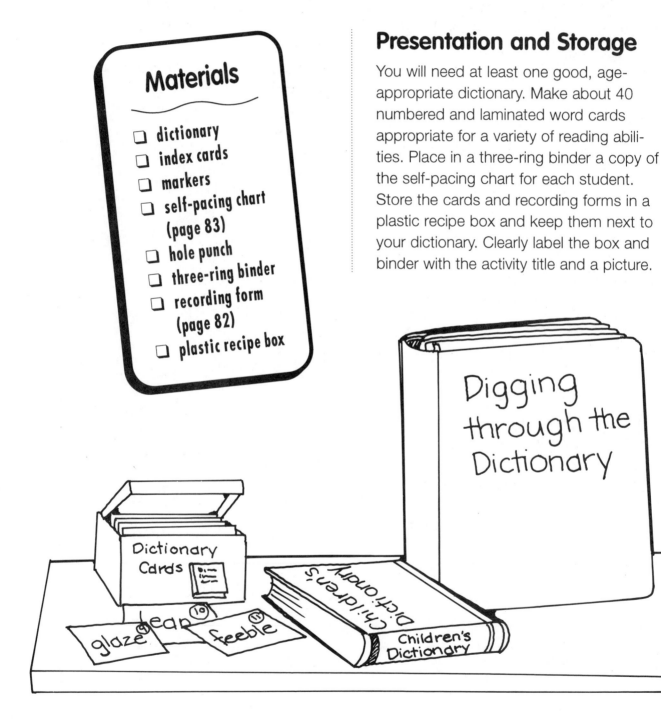

Process

Students select a card, locate the word in the dictionary, and follow the directions on the recording form. When they have completed the recording form, have students record the date on the corresponding word-card number on the self-pacing chart so that they don't repeat work. Have students place completed recording forms in the Done Tray.

Helpful Hints

The self-pacing chart is an easy reference for you and your students. You can see at a glance who's doing what by checking the binder. Although you will have made many cards for this center, do not expect children to do them all. Once a student has internalized a skill, he or she needs to be nudged toward different and more challenging experiences, applications, and contexts. Once students "get it," they need to move on to other centers. If they don't get it, they need a different approach or a different level of support.

Digging through the Dictionary

Name _Chris_   Date _Feb. 24_

My word is _Fur_

I found my word on page _95_

The guide words are

fun and _furniture_

My word means

fur is the hair That covers

an an animal's boDy.

Here's a sentence using my word:

I have E cats. They hav

lots of furr.

Digging through the Dictionary

Name _Sean_   Date _Feb. 26_

My word is _Fur_

I found my word on page _95_

The guide words are

Fun and _Furniture._

My word means

Fur is the hair that covers

an animal's body.

Here's a sentence using my word:

Do you have fur on you?

Digging through the Dictionary

Name _____ Date _____

My word is _____

I found my word on page _____

The guide words are

_____ and _____

My word means

_____

_____

_____

Here's a sentence using my word:

_____

_____

_____

_____

What Are the Other Kids Doing While You Teach Small Groups? © 1997 Creative Teaching Press

Digging through the Dictionary

Name _____

1	2	3	4	5
6	7	8	9	10
11	12	13	14	15
16	17	18	19	20
21	22	23	24	25
26	27	28	29	30
31	32	33	34	35
36	37	38	39	40

What Are the Other Kids Doing While You Teach Small Groups? © 1997 Creative Teaching Press

Expand-a-Word

Learning Objective
Using prefixes and suffixes to create new words from root words

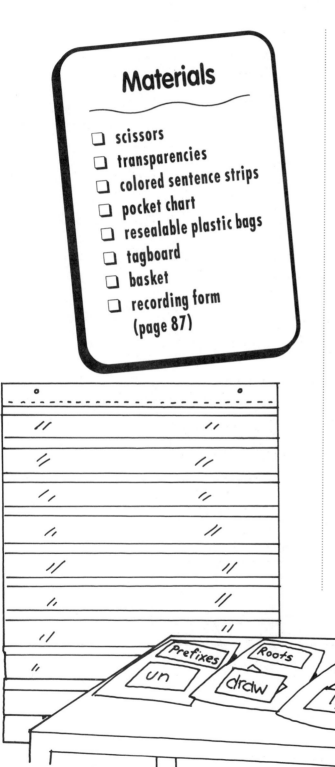

Materials

- [ ] scissors
- [ ] transparencies
- [ ] colored sentence strips
- [ ] pocket chart
- [ ] resealable plastic bags
- [ ] tagboard
- [ ] basket
- [ ] recording form (page 87)

Presentation and Storage

Cut transparencies into index-card-size pieces. On each piece, write a prefix, suffix, or root word (see sample list, page 86). These transparencies are the "hook" of this center. Students will be intrigued by the materials and will work at this center just to get to use them. Also, any time they get to use the pocket chart, students will be happy campers. Be sure to use the highest-quality, stiffest transparencies you can find. The flimsy ones will not hold up. Also provide colored sentence strips for children to use as backing in the pocket chart. Without these strips, the transparencies may be difficult to read.

Present the prefixes, suffixes, and root words in separate resealable bags. To help students return pieces to the corrects bags, list on a piece of tagboard the names of the pieces in each set and insert the tagboard into each bag. Place these bags in a small basket labeled with the activity title and a matching picture.

Process

Students place a sentence strip as a backing in the pocket chart and select a root word transparency card. Children then experiment with prefix and suffix cards to create expanded words. If a created word sounds right, children write it on the recording form. Invite students to make as many expanded words as possible with each root word.

Helpful Hints

Transparencies have a few advantages over sentence strips or index cards. They allow

- prefixes and suffixes to attach tightly to the root words.

- a student to use overlays, for example, when students need to drop a *y* and add an *i*.

- a center to be presented as a pocket chart activity or an overhead projector activity.

Expand-a-Word

Write
root word

1. Writes
2. Writeing
3. rewrite
4. writer
5. prewriting
6.
7.
8.
9.
10.

Name Joel
Date 15th

Expand-a-Word Sample List

Prefixes

pre-	un-	dis-	in-
re-	de-	mis-	be-

Root Words

eat	watch	laugh	do
push	draw	point	quiet
stand	read	walk	fast
jump	write	act	hope
build	kick	like	door
look	take	cook	side

Suffixes

-er	-es	-ing	-ed
-ful	-s	-less	-ly

What Are the Other Kids Doing While You Teach Small Groups? © 1997 Creative Teaching Press

Expand-a-Word

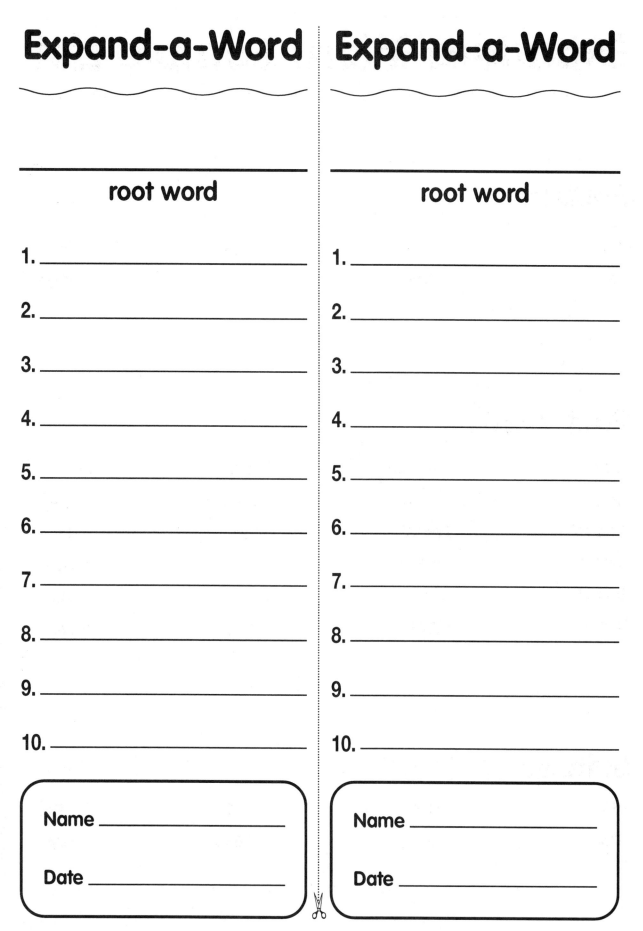

Expand-a-Word

root word

1. _____
2. _____
3. _____
4. _____
5. _____
6. _____
7. _____
8. _____
9. _____
10. _____

Name _____

Date _____

Expand-a-Word

root word

1. _____
2. _____
3. _____
4. _____
5. _____
6. _____
7. _____
8. _____
9. _____
10. _____

Name _____

Date _____

Handwriting

Learning Objective

Printing neatly and efficiently

Materials

- [ ] index cards
- [ ] markers
- [ ] glue
- [ ] handwritten alphabet
- [ ] large plastic box
- [ ] plastic stand (optional)

Presentation and Storage

Prepare a set of 30 or so handwriting cards based on published rhymes and short poems. Color-code the cards using the green-yellow-red system (see page 55) so students can choose appropriate levels. Make green cards one-line rhymes such as *Yak with a pack.* Make yellow cards very short poems and red cards more complex poems. On the back of each card, glue a copy of the handwritten alphabet for student reference. Laminate the cards. Present the cards in a large plastic box with a snap-on lid.

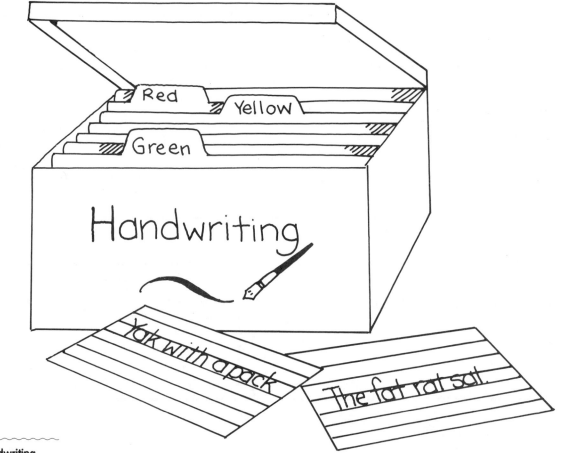

Process

Students select appropriate cards using the color-code system and carefully copy the rhymes or poems onto lined paper. Have them read their work to a friend before placing it in the Done Tray.

Helpful Hints

Make several types of lined paper available to children so they can choose paper that is appropriate for them. Light Write (page 97) should precede this activity. In Light Write, students practice forming individual letters. Letter formation is a skill that should be internalized before proceeding to this much more demanding curriculum.

You may wish to display the directions to this learning center on a plastic stand. These directions are not so much for the children as they are for parent volunteers, substitute teachers, student teachers, and visitors. The actual text for the directions is as follows.

1. *Choose a card from the file box. Use the colors to help you decide which card to choose:*
   green = hard
   yellow = harder
   red = hardest
2. *Copy the words onto lined paper. Use your very best handwriting.*
3. *Read your work to a friend or grownup and get it signed off.*

Independent Writing

Learning Objective

Practicing process-writing and continuing writing activities

Materials

- ☐ writing materials
- ☐ folders

Presentation and Storage

This center is an extension of your writing workshop or process-writing time. The materials are not separate from those used in process-writing activities—writing folders, writing paper, and pencils. Give students different-colored folders to hold their writing, and store the folders in a convenient central location. A wide variety of colors will help students locate their folders quickly and easily.

Process

Students who do this activity as a Choice are usually either anxious to finish a first draft; involved in editing a piece for publication; excited to work on their final copies; or have just gotten such a fabulous idea for a poem, joke, or story, that they can't possibly wait until the next writing time. The processes used at this center should be the same as those taught and practiced during writing-workshop or process-writing lessons.

Helpful Hints

You might try limiting writing time in your writing workshop to maximize student enthusiasm. Consider organizing your writing time as follows:

- Mini-lesson: 5–10 minutes
- Independent writing: 20 minutes
- Response and sharing: 5–10 minutes

Keeping the writing time brief leaves students just a little bit hungry for writing. This seems much better than seeing a lot of students sprawled out on their desks exhausted from extended bouts of writing. Some children, however, are developmentally ready to write for much longer periods of time. The Independent Writing center is excellent for these students.

Let's Do Lunch

Learning Objective

Reading a menu, recognizing coins, counting money, making change, staying within a budget, adding, subtracting, and writing a bill

Materials

- ☐ restaurant menus
- ☐ restaurant order forms
- ☐ props
- ☐ play money
- ☐ task cards (pages 94–95)
- ☐ plastic basket
- ☐ recording form (page 96)

Presentation and Storage

Collect menus from local restaurants. Laminated plastic menus are far more durable and motivational than disposable paper ones. Most restaurants will donate menus if you tell them you are a teacher. Purchase restaurant order forms from business-supply stores and add them to the center as well. Also, invite students to add props such as aprons, calculators, and items from a playhouse or cooking area. Realistic-looking play money and a toy cash register are also excellent additions to this center.

The task cards are designed to guide students toward skill-building while leaving the "game" open-ended. (Feel free to create your own task cards, if you wish.) Present the basic materials (menus, ordering forms, and task cards) in a plastic basket clearly marked with the activity title and a picture.

Process

When implementing this center you can have children choose their own task cards, you can assign a specific task card to a student, or you can place a new card at the center each week. The task cards are designed to guide students toward specific skills (making change, staying within a budget, and so on) without being too structured. Invite students to select the props, decide who will play each role, and select where they want to pretend they are eating. Each task card is designed to leave some evidence of student work, in the form of a picture, bill, or recording form.

Helpful Hints

Is this a math center or a literacy center? In addition to lots of opportunities for reading, writing, listening, speaking, and artistic expression, math skills such as addition, subtraction, and problem solving are also embedded in this activity. This is a good opportunity to integrate math into your Literacy Workshop! This is also a great center for students to use after completing math assignments.

Let's Do Lunch

Task Card #1

Pretend you are in a restaurant. Decide who is going to be the customer, the waiter, the cashier, the hostess, and the chef. When you are done, draw a picture of who played with you. Label your picture with everyone's job.

✂ ··

Let's Do Lunch

Task Card #2

Pretend you are in a restaurant. You are the waiter or waitress. Write down the customer's order on your pad. Be sure to include the price of each item and total the bill. Turn in the order form when you are done playing.

✂ ··

Let's Do Lunch

Task Card #3

Pretend you are in a restaurant. Take some money from the money jar. When you are done, use a recording form to report

1) what you ordered.
2) how much money your meal cost.
3) how much change you received.

What Are the Other Kids Doing While You Teach Small Groups? © 1997 Creative Teaching Press

Let's Do Lunch
Task Card #4

Pretend you are in a restaurant. Take a lot of coins from the money jar (no bills). Order a healthy breakfast. When you are done, use a recording form to report

1) what you ordered.

2) how much money your meal cost.

3) how much change you received.

Let's Do Lunch
Task Card #5

Pretend you are in a restaurant. Take exactly $5.75 from the money jar. Order lunch. Spend as close to $5.75 as possible, but don't spend more! When you are done, use a recording form to report

1) what you ordered.

2) how much your meal cost.

3) how much change you received.

Let's Do Lunch
Task Card #6

Pretend you are in a restaurant. Take a lot of money from the money jar. Take a friend out to dinner. When you are done eating, use a recording form to report

1) what you ordered.

2) how much money your meals cost.

3) how much change you received.

What Are the Other Kids Doing While You Teach Small Groups? © 1997 Creative Teaching Press

Let's Do Lunch Recording Form

Name _____ Date _____

I ordered:

It cost:

My change was:

What Are the Other Kids Doing While You Teach Small Groups? © 1997 Creative Teaching Press

Light Write

Learning Objective
Printing neatly and efficiently

Materials

- ❑ transparencies
- ❑ handwriting workbook
- ❑ overhead projector
- ❑ file folders
- ❑ magazine box
- ❑ plastic bin
- ❑ overhead pens

Presentation and Storage

Photocopy pages from a handwriting workbook onto overhead transparencies. Place transparencies in file folders clearly labeled with the appropriate letters so students can later return the transparencies to the right folders. Store the file folders in a magazine box next to the overhead projector. Leave a plastic bin filled with overhead pens near the projector as well. Working on the overhead projector makes handwriting, a sometimes laborious subject area, quite a bit more inviting to students.

Process

Invite students to choose any transparency and follow the directions from the handwriting workbook. Have them place completed transparencies in the Done Tray. Later on, choose a student to wash and dry the transparencies. Assign another student to file them alphabetically in the folders the next morning. (Not coincidentally, this job provides good alphabetizing practice!)

Helpful Hints

Have students visit this center many times before graduating to Handwriting (page 88). This center focuses on single letters; Handwriting focuses on short verses.

Making the overhead projector available to students gives rise to potential behavior issues. Students are completely fascinated by the overhead projector, transparencies, and overhead pens. This fascination sometimes leads to, shall we say, "experimentation." Despite careful and repeated modeling that sets the tone for appropriate conduct, even the most conscientious students are sometimes prone to a bit of experimentation. The best deterrent for inappropriate use of the projector is the screen. If the entire class is able to see this experimentation, it is more likely to be avoided or snuffed out quickly. Either you will catch it with your "teacher's eye," or another child will report what is happening. It takes a bit of courage to let children use the overhead, but it's well worth it.

Listening Post

Learning Objective

Reading self-selected literature for enjoyment
Listening to modeled expressive reading

Materials

- ☐ cassette players
- ☐ books with corresponding cassettes
- ☐ resealable plastic bags
- ☐ magazine box
- ☐ recording forms (pages 101–102)

Presentation and Storage

Many listening centers have at least four copies of any particular book and accompanying cassette. However, this Listening Post center requires only one copy of each book. You shouldn't find traffic problems because children should be perfectly capable of sharing materials and they have so many center options from which to select. Make available eight to ten books and corresponding tapes at a time and rotate them monthly. Store each book-and-tape set in a resealable bag and store the bags in a magazine box.

Process

Have students listen to the tape of their choice while following along in the book. Instruct them to fill out a recording form when they have finished. Two forms are included—one for fluent writers and one for less fluent writers. Children typically choose the form that is appropriate for them.

Helpful Hints

One helpful twist to the traditional listening-center setup is to get rid of the headsets! With headsets, students have a tendency to

- turn the volume up to the danger point.
- torture neighbors by turning their volume up to the danger point.
- play "Airplane Pilot."
- tie up the headset cords until they become a single, indistinguishable unit.

Without headsets, none of these behaviors is possible!

Listening Post

Name _____   Date _____

Title _____

Author _____

I thought this book was

Great **Okay** **Yuck**

because _____

_____

_____

✂ ┈┈┈

Listening Post

Name _____   Date _____

Title _____

Author _____

I thought this book was

Great **Okay** **Yuck**

because _____

_____

_____

Listening Post

Name _____ Date _____

I listened to

_____

Here is a picture of my favorite part.

Make-a-Book

Learning Objective

Practicing writing fluency through self-selected topics

Materials

- ☐ plastic basket
- ☐ blank books
- ☐ writing and illustrating materials

Presentation and Storage

This is another very easy center to set up. Just fill a basket with blank books and writing and illustrating materials. That's it! Since this center is completely open-ended, students will take care of the rest.

Process

Students love making "real" books. During the writing workshop, they have to go through many steps before they can publish—pre-writing, drafting, peer conferencing, revising, peer editing, teacher conferencing, and finally, publishing. This center offers a more expedient and less formal way for children to write and illustrate their pieces without detracting from the emphasis on writing as a process as taught during the writing workshop. All they have to do is write and illustrate stories in blank books in any way they wish.

Helpful Hints

Make all writing and art supplies easily accessible. This includes colored pencils, staplers, tape, tissue paper, construction paper, felt-tipped markers, paint, and paintbrushes. The primary objective in offering centers in the first place is to have students engaged in meaningful, independent learning while you work with small groups. If students have to interrupt you to ask *May I use your stapler?*, *Where is the green paper?*, or *I need some tape!*, your quality teaching time has been interrupted, and the students are not working independently. Completed books make great additions to your class library.

Map Attack

Learning Objective

Understanding the function and structure of maps and gathering information from them

Materials

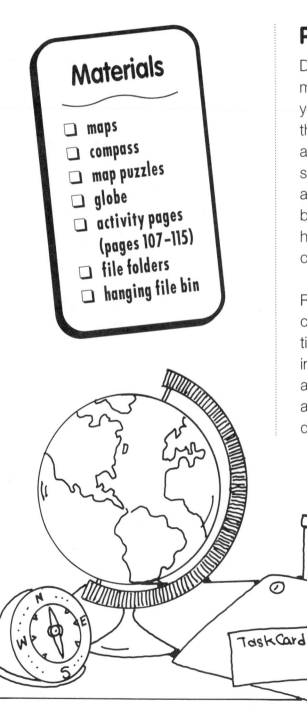

- ❑ maps
- ❑ compass
- ❑ map puzzles
- ❑ globe
- ❑ activity pages (pages 107–115)
- ❑ file folders
- ❑ hanging file bin

Presentation and Storage

Develop this curriculum around a series of maps. You may wish to include maps of your school, your city, a nearby park, a theme park, your country, your continent, and the world, as well as maps of story settings. Map puzzles and a globe are also nice additions. This center works best as a stationary poster center. If you have space, mount maps on both walls of a corner of your classroom.

Reproduce the nine activity pages and create task cards based on the suggestions on page 106. Present the map tasks in numbered file folders and store them in a hanging file bin. This center makes an attractive and functional bulletin board display as well as a useful center.

Process

The steps for completing tasks are detailed on each task card. Because the tasks on the activity pages become progressively more difficult, if you choose to have students complete them, have them do so in sequential order.

In addition to the reproducible activities, have students complete tasks such as the following:

- *Use a world map. Find the largest continent, the largest island, the largest country, the largest ocean, and the tallest mountain in the world.*

- *Use an atlas that shows the resources of the United States. List ten different farm crops and the states in which they are grown.*

- *Use a map of your state. Name three bodies of water. Name three cities near the border. Name the capital city. Name a city you have visited. What are this city's coordinates?*

- *Use a globe. What color is water on the globe? Is all the water the same color? Find some land. What color is it? Is all land the same color? Is your city north or south of the equator? If you dug a hole straight down through the earth starting at your city, where would you come out?*

Helpful Hints

After students complete five Map Attack activities, allow them a free choice. Free choices may include completing geography puzzles and map games or drawing their own maps.

Map Attack

Name _____   **Date** _____

This is a compass. You use it to find direction. A compass always points north. Use a compass to do this activity.

List three things on the north wall of the class.

_____

_____

List three things on the south wall of the class.

_____

_____

List three things on the east wall of the class.

_____

_____

List three things on the west wall of the class.

_____

_____

Map Attack

Name _____ Date _____

Use the map below for this activity.

1. Put your finger on the park.
Go two blocks south.
Go one block east.
Where are you?

_____

2. Put your finger on the pool.
Go one block east.
Go two blocks north.
Where are you?

_____

3. Which direction is the library?

_____

4. Which direction is the vacant lot?

_____

5. Which direction is the car wash?

_____

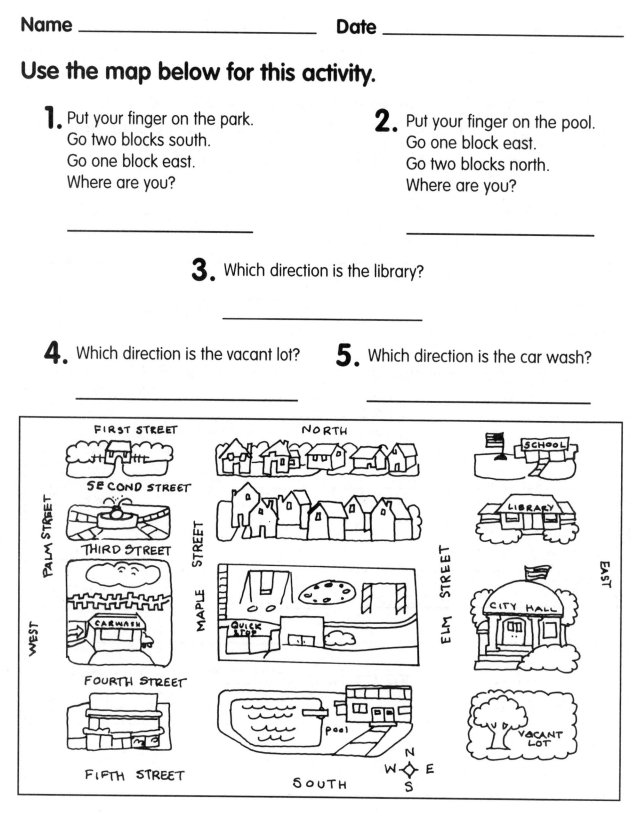

Map Attack

Name _____ Date _____

Use a pencil to trace a path on this map.
Follow the directions carefully.

1. Start at the house in the northwest corner of the map. This is your home.

2. Go down Palm Street to the car wash.

3. Turn east on Fourth Street.

4. Continue east on Fourth Street to City Hall.

5. Go north on Elm Street until you get to the school.

6. Stop to visit your friend's house on the corner of Maple Street and Second Street.

7. Go home.

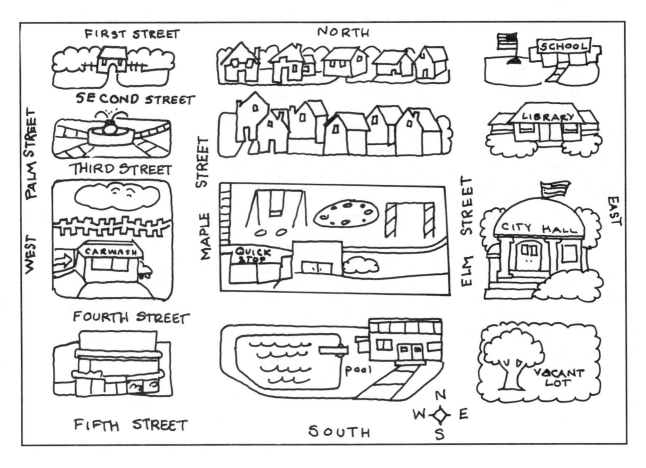

Map Attack

Name _____ **Date** _____

Use the school map below to answer these questions.

1. What is east of the drinking fountain? _____

2. What is west of the school building? _____

3. What is north of the tetherball court? _____

4. What is south of the parking lot? _____

5. What is west of the monkey bars? _____

6. What is in the southeast corner? _____

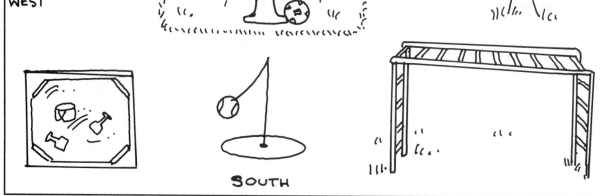

Map Attack

Name _____ Date _____

Many maps have coordinates to help you find places. Use the grid to practice using coordinates to find specific locations.

1. Place a red circle on coordinate (C, 4).

2. Place an orange X on coordinate (H, 7).

3. Place a blue dot on coordinate (E, 3).

4. Place a happy face on coordinate (B, 6).

5. Place a star on coordinate (F, 5).

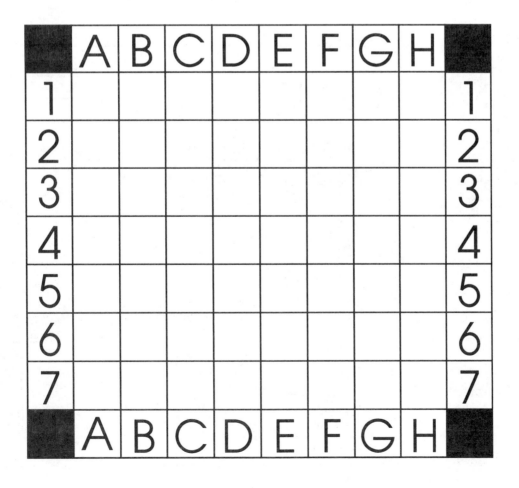

Map Attack

Name _____ Date _____

Describe the locations of these places using their coordinate positions.

1. Where is the car wash? _____

2. Where is the swingset? _____

3. Where is the flagpole? _____

4. Where is the fountain? _____

Map Attack

Name _____ **Date** _____

Use the United States map below for this activity.

1. Color California red.

2. Put a brown X on Texas.

3. Make a green circle around Florida.

4. Put an orange X on Hawaii.

5. Color Alaska blue.

6. Put a purple star on Maine.

7. Name three states that touch Mexico.

_____   _____   _____

8. Name three states that touch Canada.

_____   _____   _____

9. Name three states that touch the Pacific Ocean.

_____   _____   _____

10. Name three states that touch the Atlantic Ocean.

_____   _____   _____

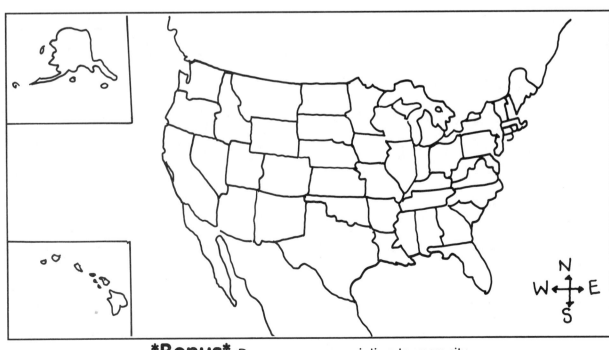

Bonus Draw an arrow pointing to your city.

Map Attack

Name _____   Date _____

This is a map of North America. It is divided into countries.
Color Canada, the United States, and Mexico.

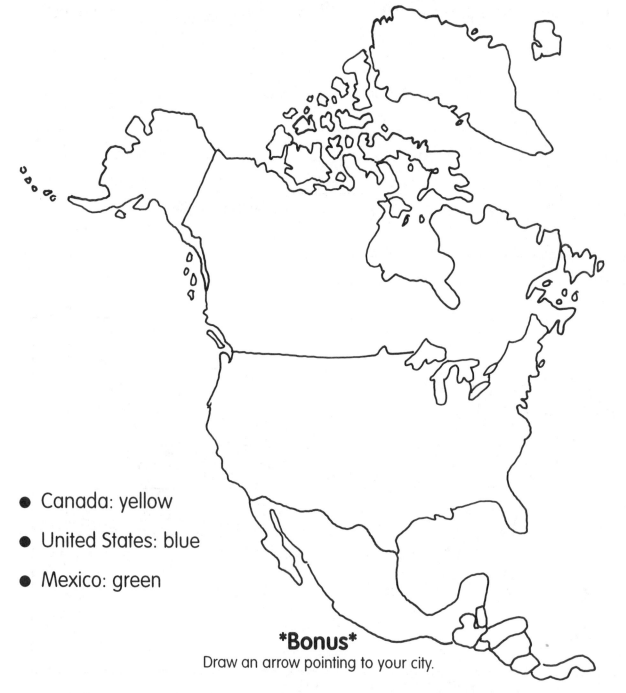

- Canada: yellow

- United States: blue

- Mexico: green

Bonus
Draw an arrow pointing to your city.

Map Attack

Name _____ **Date** _____

Use this map of the continents to answer these questions.

1. How many continents are there?

_____

2. On which continent do you live?

_____

3. Which continent is the smallest?

_____

4. What three continents are connected?

_____

_____

_____

5. What do you think a continent is?

_____

_____

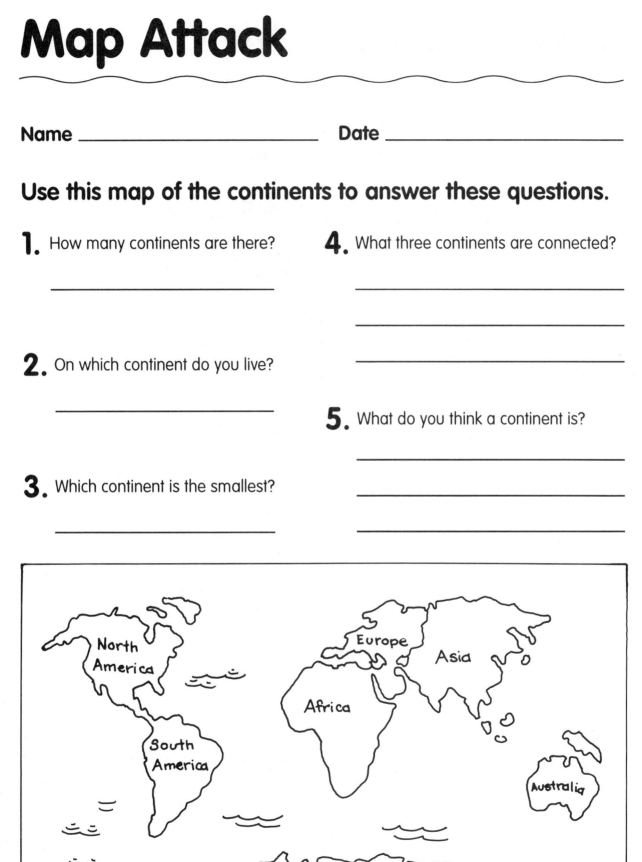

Never-Ending Story

Learning Objective

Sustaining a cumulative and collaborative piece of creative writing

Materials

- ☐ three-ring binder
- ☐ recording form (page 118)
- ☐ hole punch

Presentation and Storage

Collect student contributions to the Never-Ending Story and organize them in a three-ring binder. Use the recording forms to maintain uniform-looking pages. The notebook takes virtually no space; keep it on a shelf with other small centers. Store recording forms in the children's classroom "office."

Process

This center is designed for fairly advanced writers. It becomes increasingly difficult as the year progresses, matching the progress students are making. The first writer begins the story without limitations or rules, except that the story must be appropriate for school and neatly written. The next writer reads the first writer's piece and continues the story in a logical, sequential manner. The third writer reads the other two writers' pieces and continues the story. As the story becomes longer, it also becomes increasingly more difficult because there is more reading involved. As students complete pages, have them place their work in the Done Tray so you can hole-punch it for binding. At the end of the year, bind the Never-Ending Story into a book and keep it in your class library.

Helpful Hints

Read the Never-Ending Story aloud to the class periodically to motivate students to participate. If students notice spelling errors or other mistakes in their classmates' work, invite them to either tactfully point them out or to ignore them. The point of this center is to create a story that is spontaneous and collaborative rather than one that is perfect and publishable.

Never-Ending Story

_____

_____

_____

_____

_____

_____

Name _____ **Date** _____ **Page** _____

Newspaper

Learning Objective

Gaining familiarity with newspapers and reading for information

Materials

- newspapers
- task cards (pages 121–122)
- index cards
- tray

Presentation and Storage

You will need ongoing access to newspapers for this center. Either ask your local newspaper about subscription donations or ask families to donate their newspapers after reading them. (Request that newspapers be refolded so students can learn to navigate them.) You might also consider writing a grant for a class subscription or making an appeal to community partners. You don't need a class set of papers for this center. Four to six copies work just fine. Stack newspapers on a shelf and recycle them each week so you never have more than ten newspapers at a time. Copy and cut apart the task cards or create some of your own, and store them in a small tray on top of the newspapers.

Process

Students choose a task card and use the newspaper to find and record information. The skills covered by the task cards cover common newspaper sections and address a range of curriculum areas. This is an excellent center for integrating other subject areas.

Helpful Hints

Don't try to reuse newspapers. Many adults have trouble packing up the morning paper. Can you imagine what happens when children take the paper apart? Once a newspaper has "exploded," just recycle it.

Newspaper Task Cards

1
Make a collage of words and pictures from the newspaper that describe you.

2
Cut out three people pictures from the newspaper. Write a story about these people. Describe how they are connected with each other.

3
Find and read an advertisement. Write a paragraph to your family describing why they should or should not buy this product.

4
Cut out an interesting picture from the newspaper. Write a news story to explain it.

5
Cut out an interesting picture from the sports section. Write a sentence describing what happened just before this picture was taken.

6
Write your own answer to a Dear Abby letter.

Newspaper Task Cards

7

Look through the sports section. Cut out at least ten action words and glue them on a sheet of construction paper. Write five more action words yourself.

8

Rewrite a headline using your own words.

9

Find a picture of an animal. Write as many adjectives as you can to describe this animal.

10

Find and read a story about a hero. Write a story about a hero you know.

11

Look through the classified ads. Find items you'd like to buy and list their names and prices.

12

List today's weather in five different cities.

Overhead Projector

Learning Objective

Reading poems with fluency and expression

Materials

- ☐ transparencies
- ☐ overhead projector
- ☐ cellophane tape
- ☐ cardboard frames, file folders, or plastic sleeves
- ☐ magazine storage box
- ☐ recording form (page 125)
- ☐ magnetic clip

Presentation and Storage

Make overhead transparencies of the poems you study in your Book Clubs. This set of poems will increase as the year progresses. A good way to present the transparencies is to tape them onto transparency frames. These cardboard frames are quite durable and help to keep dirty little fingers off the film. If you are unable to find these, store transparencies in file folders or plastic sleeves. Store the frames, folders, or plastic sleeves in a labeled magazine storage box.

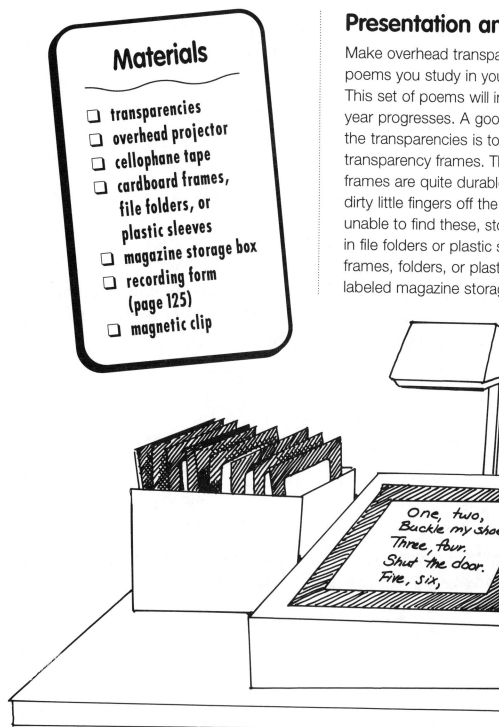

One, two,
Buckle my shoe.
Three, four.
Shut the door.
Five, six,

Process

Students read aloud up to five poems from the overhead and record the titles on the recording form. Consider having students read poems in pairs for accountability. Attach the half-sheet recording forms to the overhead projector with a magnetic clip.

Helpful Hints

You may have some behavior issues with this center. Children have been known to

- play with the focus knob on the projector.

- play with the transparencies. (A seemingly fun thing for children to do is to try to read transparencies stacked on top of each other. At least that's what they say they're doing.)

- practice shadow puppets.

- project a variety of unacceptable things onto the screen.

Solve these problems by moving the overhead projector right next to your teaching corner so you can see the screen. Teacher's eyes have tangible power inside a classroom.

Be sure all the poems presented at this center have been practiced, chanted, sung, and acted out during Book Clubs. This level of familiarity is necessary for students to work at this center independently.

Overhead Projector

Name _____ Date _____

1. _____

2. _____

3. _____

4. _____

5. _____

✂ ···

Overhead Projector

Name _____ Date _____

1. _____

2. _____

3. _____

4. _____

5. _____

What Are the Other Kids Doing While You Teach Small Groups? © 1997 Creative Teaching Press

Post Office

Learning Objective

Writing friendly letters and addressing envelopes

Materials

- ❑ stationery
- ❑ envelopes
- ❑ tiered metal shelf
- ❑ small cardboard organizer
- ❑ blank postcards

Presentation and Storage

Provide several different "levels" of stationery to match students' writing abilities. Include some paper with wide lines and lots of space for illustrations and other paper with narrow lines and no space for illustrations. Correctly address and laminate a large envelope as a model. Provide business-size envelopes for young writers who print in giant-size letters.

A good way to store this center is in a tiered metal shelf that holds stacks of stationery. Use a small cardboard organizer to store envelopes. Include some postcards for variety.

Process

Students write a letter and properly address an envelope. Have an adult classroom helper check the letters for spelling and propriety, or have students place letters in the Done Tray to be checked later. A real mailbox is a great complement for this center. Finished letters can be tossed in the mailbox. Each week, give a different student the responsibility of delivering the mail.

Helpful Hints

Make a list (with photos) of staff members who agree to write letters back to students. This guaranteed response motivates students and makes the activity authentic. Of course, do not limit students to writing just to these people. Students may want to write to the President, Santa Claus, classmates, family members, and famous actors and athletes.

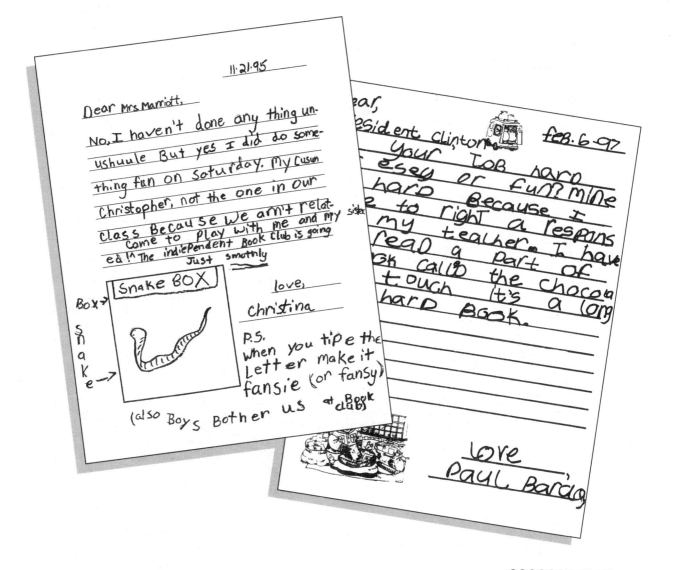

Reading to Learn

Learning Objective

Accessing and reporting information using content-area books
Gaining awareness of book parts (table of contents, glossary, index)

Materials

- reproducible task card (page 131)
- cardstock
- nonfiction books
- large resealable plastic bags
- large bin
- construction paper

Presentation and Storage

Laminate sturdy cardstock copies of the reproducible to create a set of task cards that correspond to specific book selections. (See page 130 for a list of recommended nonfiction resources.) Write in each section of the card a question or topic addressed in the book's text. For example, in the four boxes of a task card on weather, you might write *Different Kinds of Weather*, *What Makes Snow?*, *What Makes Rain?*, and *My Favorite Weather*. Number the cards sequentially from easiest book to hardest. Present each card in a large resealable bag with the corresponding book and activity materials. Store the entire set of bags in a large bin.

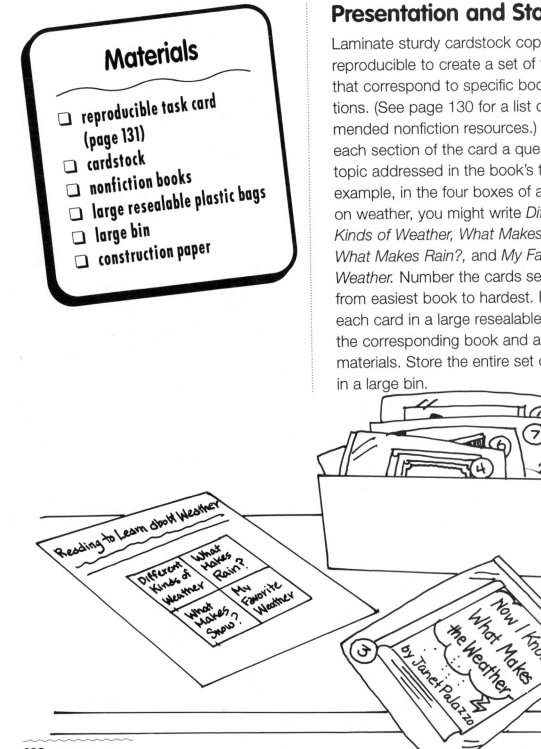

Process

Students choose topics from the task cards, working sequentially through the set. The first books should be short and easy to read. As students progress through the cards, books and tasks should require students to use the table of contents, index, and skimming techniques to locate information. Have students use a four-square poster format (similar to the format on the reproducible) to report on the topics listed on each task card. Most students will probably want to use a large sheet of construction paper divided into four quadrants, but some may choose other methods, such as taping together four different-colored sheets of construction paper.

Helpful Hints

This center's objective is to introduce students to research processes. Children should

- use a variety of nonfiction books.
- learn to read for a purpose.
- learn to locate information.
- report information in writing.

Include corresponding books with task cards because this center is not intended to have students actually locate resources. This comes later, in the Research center (page 132). Although this center is not dependent on having these exact titles, the resource list on page 130 will help you get started. Use this learning center to integrate science into your language arts block.

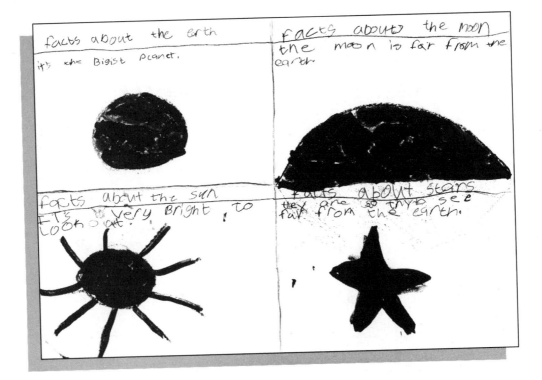

Reading to Learn Resource List

Air	Branley, Franklyn. *Air Is All around You.* Harper & Row. 1986.
Ants	Selsam, Millicent E. *Questions and Answers about Ants.* Scholastic. 1991.
Bees	Eastman, David. *I Can Read about Bees and Wasps.* Troll. 1979.
Butterflies	Chinery, Michael. *Life Story: Butterfly.* Troll. 1991.
California	Ross, Wilma, S. *Fabulous Facts about the 50 States.* Scholastic. 1991.
Clouds	DePaola, Tomie. *The Cloud Book.* Holiday House. 1985.
Dinosaurs	Eastman, David. *Now I Know: The Story of Dinosaurs.* Troll. 1983.
Dogs	White, Nancy. *Why Do Dogs Do That?* Scholastic. 1995.
Electricity	Bains, Rae. *Discovering Electricity.* Troll. 1982.
Origami	Sarasas, Claude. *The ABC's of Origami.* Tuttle. 1984.
Plants	Gibbons, Gail. *From Seed to Plant.* Holiday House. 1991.
Quicksand	DePaola, Tomie. *The Quicksand Book.* Holiday House. 1984.
Rocks	Podendorf, Illa. *Rocks and Minerals.* Childrens Press. 1982.
Snakes	Shapp, Martha and Charles. *Let's Find Out about Snakes.* Franklin Watts. 1977.
Space	Moche, Dinah, L. *My First Book about Space.* Goldencraft. 1982.
Spiders	Merrians, Deborah. *I Can Read about Spiders.* Troll. 1997.
Weather	Palazzo, Janet. *What Makes the Weather.* Troll. 1988.
Whales	Milton, Joyce. *Whales: The Gentle Giants.* Random House. 1989.
World Records	McWhirter, Norris. *Guinness Book of World Records.* Bantam. 1996.
The Zoo	Rinard, Judith E. *What Happens at the Zoo?* National Geographic Society. 1984.

Reading to Learn about _____

Read the book about _____. You may read alone or
with a friend. Then, make a four-square poster report labeled like this
task card. Be sure to use words and pictures. Have fun!

Research

Learning Objective

Posing a set of research questions, locating materials, accessing information, and publishing a report

Materials

- research proposal form (page 134)
- library pass
- research materials

Presentation and Storage

This is the most independent center in this program. The goal is that students will learn to find their own materials in the library on topics that are interesting or important to them. All you need to provide are research proposal forms and a library pass. Arranging to have research materials available in the classroom may limit students' options. You may want to offer a selection of nonfiction books in your room to get students started, but be sure that research projects are not limited to these supplies. The potential at this center for meaningful growth and learning is tremendous.

Process

Students begin this multi-day project by completing a proposal. They need to do some pre-thinking about what they want to learn, how they will learn it, and how they will demonstrate and share this learning. After the proposal is approved, students work independently gathering resources, reading, and writing.

Helpful Hints

Clearly, this center is designed for more independent students. These students must be fluent readers, thoughtful processors, and responsible workers. Prior to conducting research, students should spend quite a bit of time at Reading to Learn (page 128), a center that provides important preparatory experiences. This center comes closest to truly independent learning. Students simply tell you what they want to learn and how they're going to learn it, and off they go.

Meet with student researchers every other day or so, just to check on their progress. On the bottom of the proposal form, there is a space for conference notes. Keep these conferences short and snappy—five minutes maximum! If you offer many center choices, you will seldom have more than two or three students working on independent research at any one time.

Research Proposal

Name _____ **Date** _____

Use this form to plan your research project. It's all right if your questions change as you go. Remember, research projects can take two or three weeks to complete. Be patient, work hard, and have fun!

Research Topic

_____

Research Questions

1. _____

2. _____

3. _____

4. _____

Research Materials

1. _____

2. _____

3. _____

Conference Notes

Stamp-a-Card

Learning Objective

Writing notes, invitations, and friendly letters

Materials

- ☐ rubber stamps
- ☐ stamp pads
- ☐ colored construction paper
- ☐ hardware organizer
- ☐ plastic baskets

Presentation and Storage

Take advantage of students' love for ink stamps. Stamps with messages such as *Happy Birthday, I Miss You, Congratulations, Merry Christmas, Get Well Soon, Thank You, Happy Anniversary,* and *You're Invited* are often reasonably priced. Also provide upper-case and lowercase letter stamps, number stamps, and ink pads in different colors. Make small sheets of colored construction paper available as well.

Hardware organizers for nuts, screws, and bolts are excellent stamp holders. Label the drawers with the letters of the alphabet, one letter per drawer, and put an uppercase and lowercase letter stamp in each. This makes it easy for students to find letters they need to stamp their own messages. Use the extra drawers for number stamps. Store message stamps and ink pads in a basket on top of the organizer. Store construction paper in a slightly larger basket beside it.

Process

Students use the materials to make greeting cards. Some students may choose to color the outside and stamp a message on the inside. Others may stamp a message on the outside and handwrite a personal note on the inside. Some students may even stamp messages on every available surface of the paper. Have students place completed cards in the Done Tray. Return them to the author for delivery as soon as they are checked for spelling and propriety.

Helpful Hints

You may catch students stamping incoherent gobbledygook in what looks like a stamping frenzy. Keep in mind that students need to "play" with materials a bit before they are ready to use them for learning. Consider inviting students who demonstrate a need for this playtime to come in during recess. Expect that stamps will be used during class time only for messages.

Stamp Collecting

Learning Objective

Locating countries on a map

Materials

- ☐ postage stamp grab bag
- ☐ glue
- ☐ index cards
- ☐ world maps
- ☐ large paper clip
- ☐ library-card pocket
- ☐ recording form (page 139)

Presentation and Storage

Inexpensive postage-stamp grab bags can often be found at coin and stamp stores. Using only those stamps that clearly bear the name of a country, glue each stamp onto an index card and laminate. Consider providing two maps at this center—a small plain world map and a large plastic floor map on which children can lie as they work.

This activity works best as a poster center. Poster centers are wonderful because they take absolutely no counter space! Title a poster *Stamp Collecting* and attach a small world map to it with a large paper clip. Glue on a library-card pocket for storing the stamp cards. Store the recording forms in the classroom "office." After selecting a stamp card, students can either remove the map from the poster or work with larger maps you have stored nearby.

Stamp Cards

Maps

Process

Have children take out a stamp and match it to the country on either world map. Then, have students complete the recording form. This form invites students to practice their map-reading skills by locating bodies of water and bordering countries. It also helps them build familiarity with cardinal directions.

Helpful Hints

Change the stamp cards each week to feature different countries. Number the stamp cards on the back to make this rotation easier. Also consider making many stamps available and inviting students to choose the countries or stamps most interesting to them. Students should visit this center many times before they begin Map Attack (page 105).

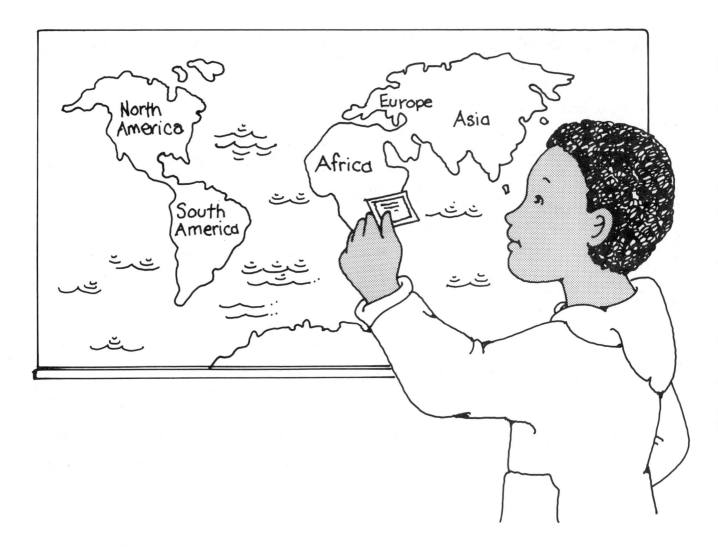

Stamp Collecting

Name _____ **Date** _____

What country is your stamp from? _____

Find the country on a world map. Then, answer these questions.

1. What bodies of water touch this country?

_____

2. What is the bordering country to the north?

_____

3. What is the bordering country to the east?

_____

4. Is this country north or south of the equator?

_____

5. Use the back of this recording form to draw a detailed picture of your stamp.

Sticker Story

Learning Objective

Using descriptive language to tell a story
Sequencing thoughts and ideas

Materials

- ☐ stickers
- ☐ recording form (page 142)
- ☐ basket
- ☐ three-ring binder
- ☐ hole punch
- ☐ transparent tape

Presentation and Storage

Provide stickers and Sticker Story recording forms in a basket. Use a three-ring notebook to display completed stories. Tape the following instructions on the front of the notebook.

1. *Write a story. Be sure to spell your spelling words correctly.*
2. *Use the stickers to help illustrate your story.*
3. *Get "grown-up" writing if you need it.*
4. *Get signed off.*
5. *Put your story in the Done Tray.*

Process

Students use stickers as story subjects and illustration tools. After checking the stories, hole-punch and insert them into the three-ring binder.

Helpful Hints

Do not limit the number of stickers children may use or tell them they must write before illustrating. You will find that the fewer rules you impose on students, the more responsibility they will assume. Since they are monitoring themselves (and each other), you should not have too many problems with sticker gluttons.

Sticker Story

by ___Liz___

Thar wz A CNTes for the BsT DAsR.

There was a contest for the best dancer.

142 Sticker Story

What Are the Other Kids Doing While You Teach Small Groups? © 1997 Creative Teaching Press

Sticker Story

by _____

by _____

What Are the Other Kids Doing While You Teach Small Groups? © 1997 Creative Teaching Press

Tape-a-Story

Learning Objective

Reading with expression and fluency

Materials

- ☐ books
- ☐ tape recorder
- ☐ blank tapes
- ☐ optional recording form (page 145)

Presentation and Storage

This is a very simple center to set up. All you need are books, a child-friendly tape recorder, and one blank tape. You could make this center more involved by including a tape in each student's literacy portfolio and having a cross-age tutor or other volunteer run the center. You may find, however, that the high maintenance takes the power away from children and strips away much of the learning. It seems that the more complicated the center, the more dependent students become. Shifting the emphasis from product to process often yields much richer learning.

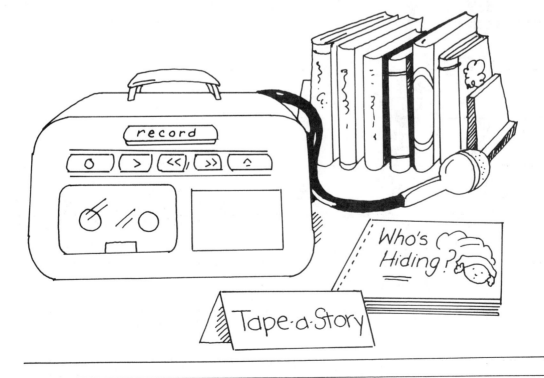

Process

Students choose a book, practice reading it at least once, and then record themselves reading it, adding appropriate sound effects as desired. Students may re-record the story as many times as necessary to produce a fluid, expressive recording. When they have made a satisfactory product, have children play the tape for a classmate or an adult. This immediate feedback is very validating to students. If no one is available to listen to the story, suggest that students place the tape in the Done Tray for review at a later time. Leave a spare tape in the center in case a student needs to turn in a recording.

Helpful Hints

Add colored stickers to the buttons on the tape recorder—a red sticker on the stop button, green stickers on the record and play buttons, and a white sticker with an arrow on the rewind button. This helps less independent readers use the tape recorder. If you wish, include recording forms at the center. You may find, though, that the recording form requires extra management. If you opt for recording sheets, still use only one blank tape. Students will more likely take greater risks and read harder books if they know the recording is temporary. Outstanding recordings can be added to the Listening Post (page 99).

Tape-a-Story

Name _____ Date _____

Date	Title and Author
1.	
2.	
3.	
4.	
5.	

Thesaurus

Learning Objective

Gaining familiarity with the function, structure, and use of a thesaurus

Presentation and Storage

In addition to a thesaurus and recording forms, include about 40 labeled, illustrated, and laminated word cards at this center (similar to Digging through the Dictionary, page 80). When selecting words from the thesaurus for these cards, choose those that have clear illustrations. Photocopy these illustrations and glue them on the cards to help your students work independently. Place in a three-ring binder a copy of the self-pacing chart for each student. Present the cards in a plastic recipe box next to the thesaurus. Keep the recording forms in the classroom "office."

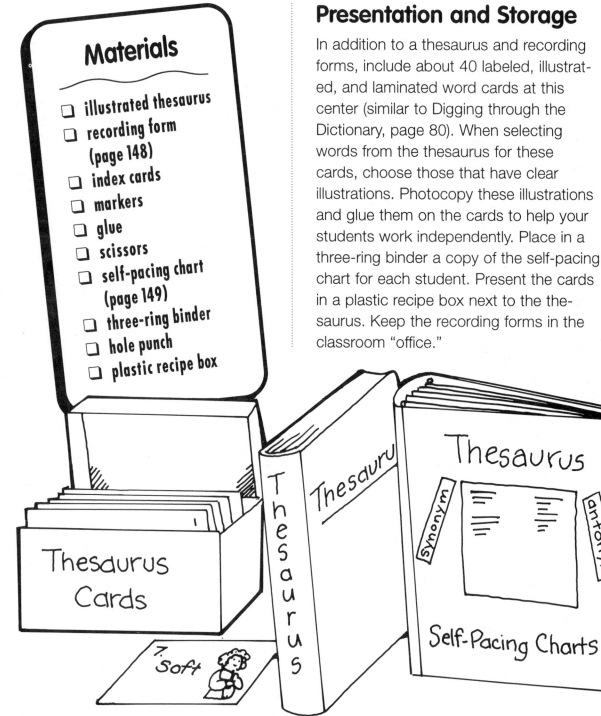

Materials

- ☐ illustrated thesaurus
- ☐ recording form (page 148)
- ☐ index cards
- ☐ markers
- ☐ glue
- ☐ scissors
- ☐ self-pacing chart (page 149)
- ☐ three-ring binder
- ☐ hole punch
- ☐ plastic recipe box

Process

A student takes a card and looks up the word in the thesaurus. The recording form asks the student to locate the word using guide words, identify available synonyms, and, most importantly, write a sentence using a synonym. When they have finished, have students record the date on the corresponding word-card space on the self-pacing chart so that they don't repeat work. Have students place completed recording forms in the Done Tray.

Helpful Hints

This center requires some very direct teaching. The student-expert model (see page 31) is most appropriate for teaching this activity, but is not enough. Students need to see "real-life" applications of using a thesaurus. Have students use the thesaurus during writing activities such as writing workshop, shared writing, guided writing, and "morning message" to provide an authentic context and application of the skills.

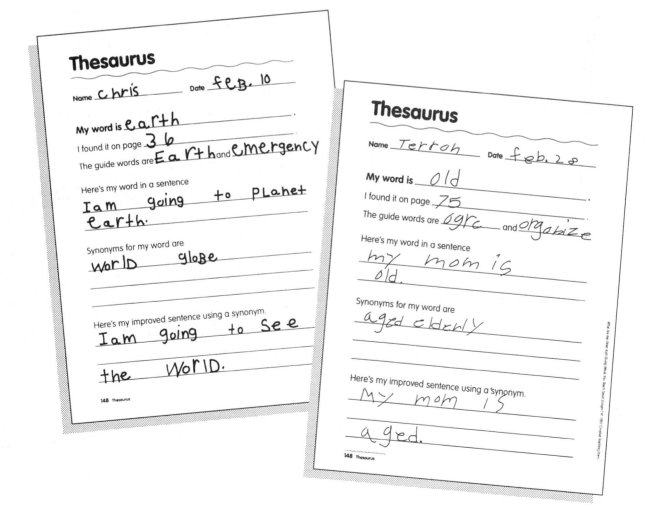

Thesaurus

Name _____ **Date** _____

My word is _____ .

I found it on page _____ .

The guide words are _____ and _____ .

Here's my word in a sentence.

_____

_____

Synonyms for my word are

_____

_____

Here's my improved sentence using a synonym.

_____

_____

What Are the Other Kids Doing While You Teach Small Groups? © 1997 Creative Teaching Press

Thesaurus Self-Pacing Chart

Name _____

1	2	3	4	5
6	7	8	9	10
11	12	13	14	15
16	17	18	19	20
21	22	23	24	25
26	27	28	29	30
31	32	33	34	35
36	37	38	39	40

Typewrite Right

Learning Objective

Gaining keyboard facility

Materials

- ☐ rhymes and poems
- ☐ colored construction paper
- ☐ electric typewriter or computer
- ☐ typing paper

Presentation and Storage

Type out several short rhymes and poems and laminate them on colored construction paper. Store them next to an electric typewriter or computer and a tray of typing paper. If you use computers, be sure students know how to operate the printer. Be sure the rhymes and poems help students practice every letter, every number, and most punctuation marks.

Mary had a little lamb.

Typing Paper

Typewrite Right

Process

Students type one of the poems or rhymes on the typewriter or computer. When introducing the center, model proper hand position and posture (wrists above fingers, feet flat on the floor, back straight). Be sure students practice proper hand position and posture as they work at the typewriter or keyboard.

Helpful Hints

A good strategy is to make sure at least one student is an expert at inserting paper into the typewriter or printer—this can be quite challenging for children. Again, if students have to interrupt you as you are teaching, they are not set up for truly independent learning. A classroom expert can save the day for you and your kids.

What happens if the machine fails? A good rule for students is that, if any machine goes down, it is simply closed for the day. A good rule for you is that nothing is more important than focusing on your Book Clubs.

Word Games

Learning Objective

Gaining familiarity with contractions and compound words

Materials

- ❑ game boards, cards, and pieces (pages 154–160)
- ❑ glue
- ❑ file folders
- ❑ plastic pencil box

Presentation and Storage

Photocopy and laminate the game boards. You can also use the blank template to create your own word games. Skills presented as games have almost instant appeal to young children. Store the game boards on top of a storage shelf and keep the game pieces in a plastic pencil box.

Process

There are many social and procedural decisions that students must make when playing games, including

- with whom to play.

- who goes first.

- where to play.

- how long to play.

- how much "helping" is allowed.

By placing these decisions in the hands of young learners, you considerably "up the ante" for learning. You may find opportunities to play these word games as part of the Book Club process. If the text introduces a contraction, invite students to play Contraction Caper 1 (page 154). By playing the game during Book Clubs, you will be modeling the decision-making skills students need for working at this center.

Helpful Hints

Make large versions of the games and laminate them or simply glue the small copies presented in this text into file folders. These smaller versions are easier to store and do not hinder the learning potential.

Directions: Place word cards facedown. Take the top card. Read the words and move your marker to the next correct contraction on the game board. The first bee to get to the hive is the winner.

Contraction Caper 1

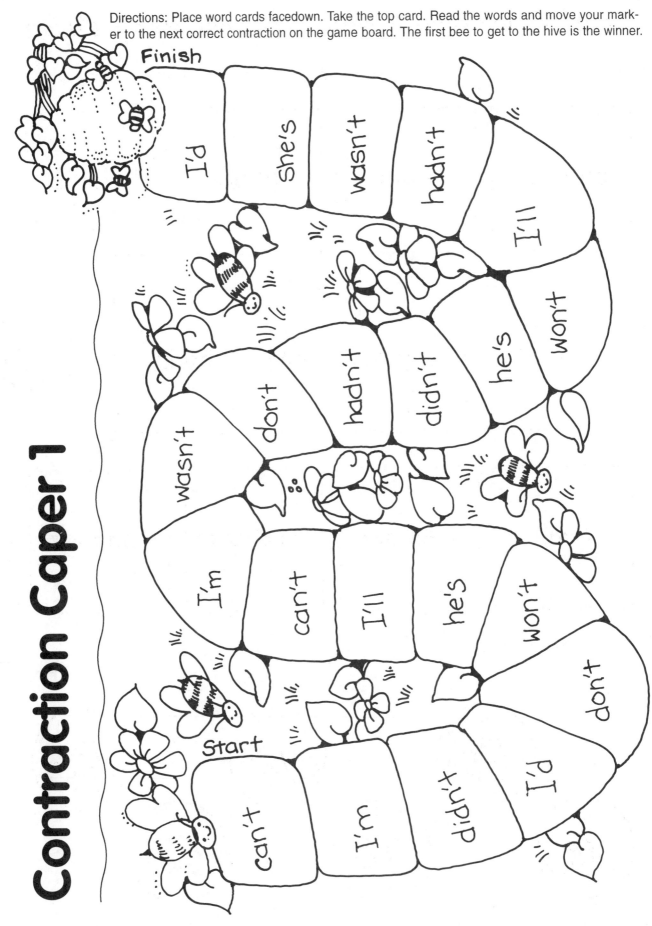

Finish

I'd She's wasn't hadn't I'll won't he's didn't hadn't don't wasn't

I'm can't I'll he's won't don't I'd

Start can't I'm didn't I'd

Contraction Caper 1: Word Cards and Game Pieces

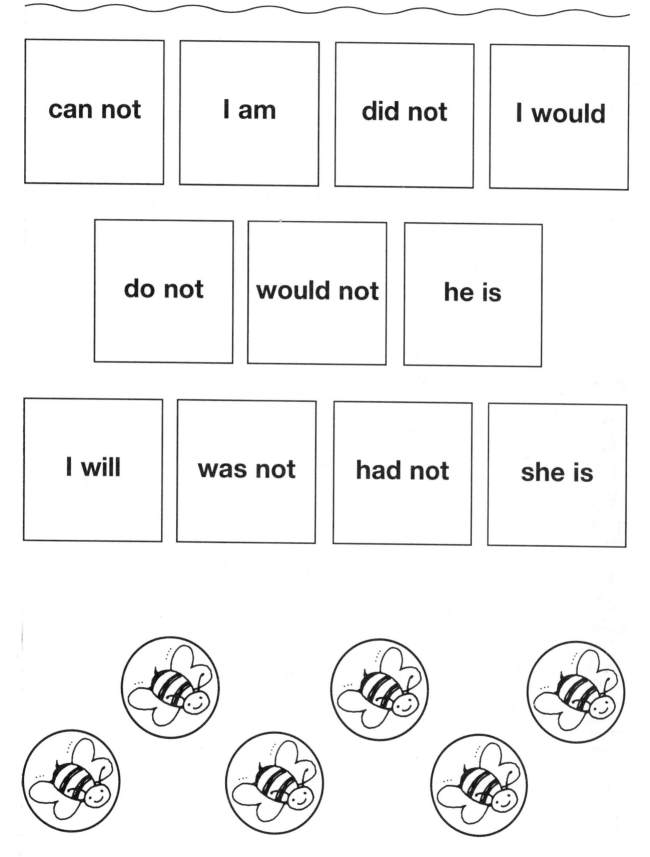

can not

I am

did not

I would

do not

would not

he is

I will

was not

had not

she is

Directions: Place word cards facedown. Take the top card. Read the words and move your marker to the next correct contraction on the game board. The first mouse to get to the cheese is the winner.

Contraction Caper 2

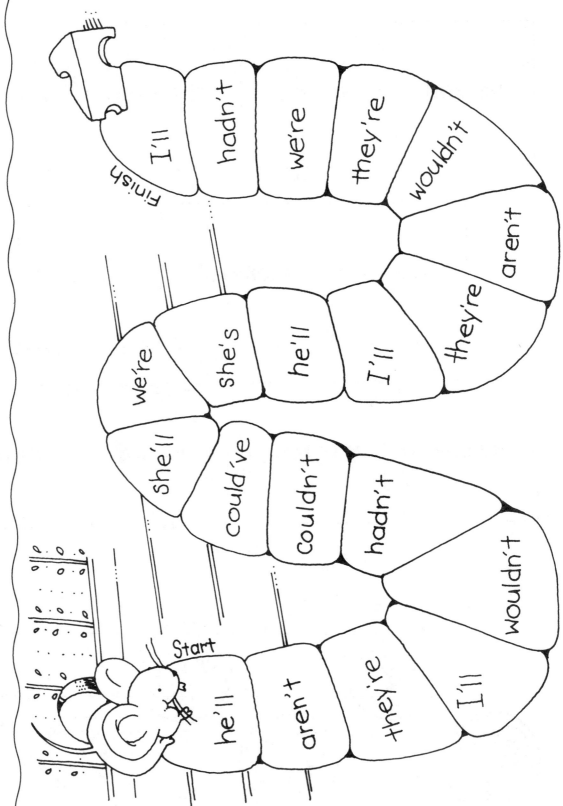

Finish

I'll · hadn't · we're · they're · wouldn't · aren't · they're · I'll · he'll · she's · we're · she'll · could've · couldn't · hadn't · wouldn't · I'll · they're · aren't · he'll

Start

Contraction Caper 2: Word Cards and Game Pieces

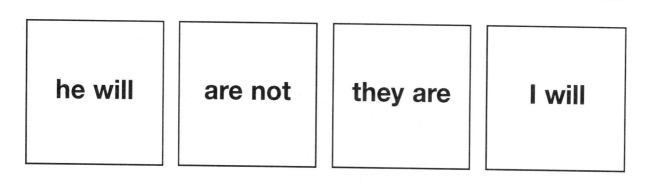

he will | are not | they are | I will

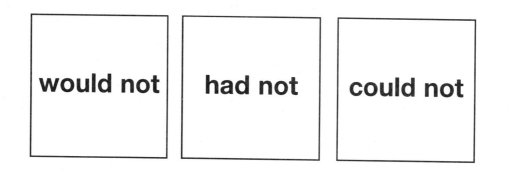

would not | had not | could not

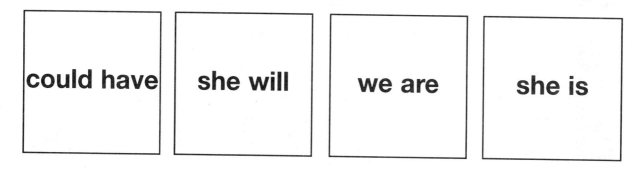

could have | she will | we are | she is

Directions: Place word cards facedown. Take the top card. Read the word and move your marker to the next opposite word on the game board. The first frog to get to the pond is the winner.

Opposites

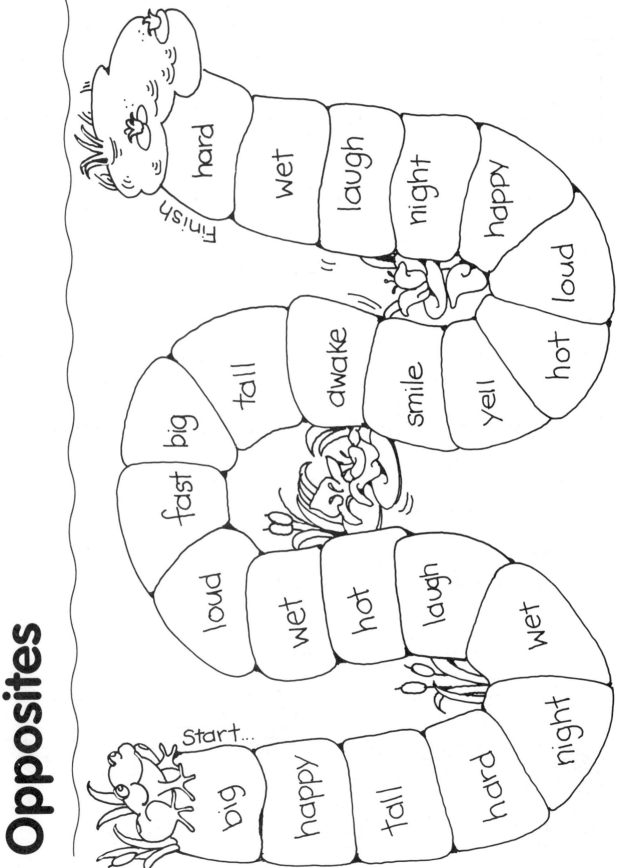

Finish

hard

wet

laugh

night

happy

loud

hot

yell

smile

awake

tall

big

fast

loud

wet

hot

laugh

wet

night

Start...

big

happy

tall

hard

What Are the Other Kids Doing While You Teach Small Groups? © 1997 Creative Teaching Press

Opposites: Word Cards and Game Pieces

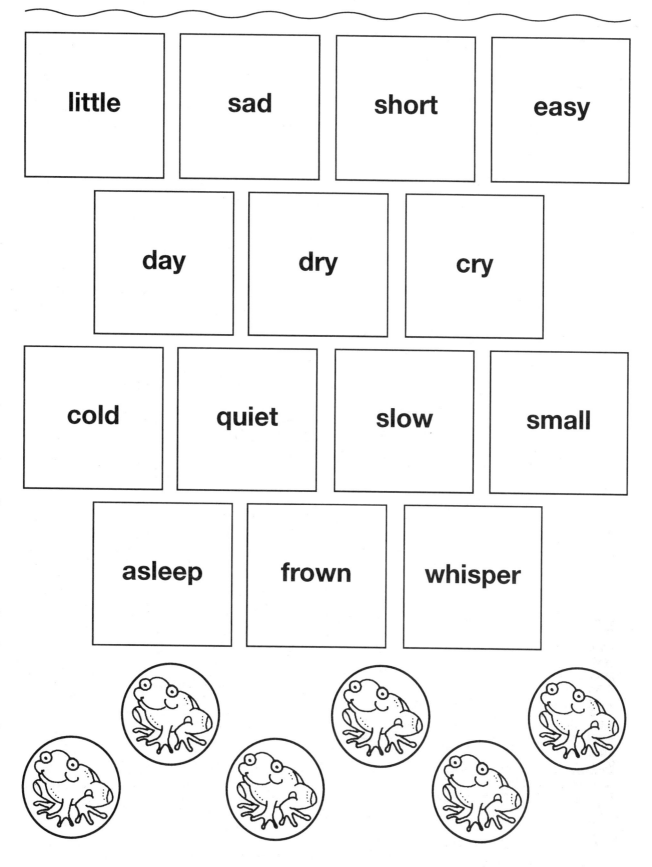

| little | sad | short | easy |

| day | dry | cry |

| cold | quiet | slow | small |

| asleep | frown | whisper |

Game Board

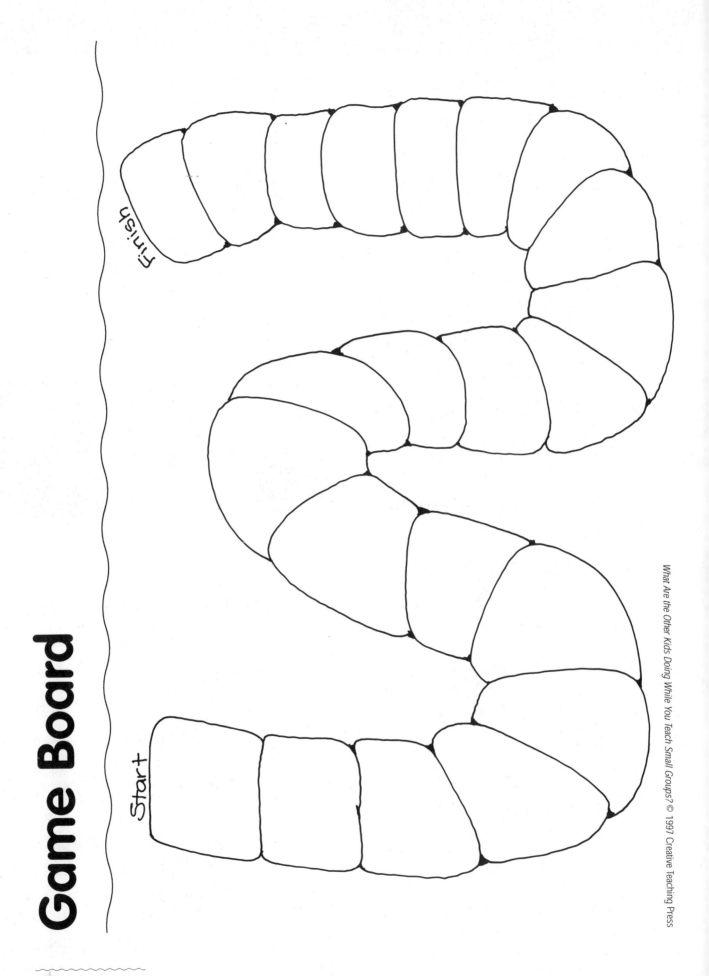

Start

Finish